Evaluator's Handbook

Joan L. Herman
Lynn Lyons Morris
Carol Taylor Fitz-Gibbon

Center for the Study of Evaluation
University of California, Los Angeles

SAGE PUBLICATIONS
The International Professional Publishers
Newbury Park   London   New Delhi

The second edition of the *Program Evaluation Kit* was developed at the Center for the Study of Evaluation, Graduate School of Education, University of California, Los Angeles.

The development of this second edition of the CSE *Program Evaluation Kit* was supported in part by a grant from the National Institute of Education, currently known as the Office of Educational Research and Improvement. However, the opinions expressed herein do not necessarily reflect the position or policy of that agency and no official endorsement should be inferred.

The second edition of the *Program Evaluation Kit* is published and distributed by Sage Publications, Inc., Newbury Park, California, under an exclusive agreement with The Regents of the University of California.

For information address:

SAGE Publications, Inc.
2455 Teller Road
Newbury Park, California 91320

SAGE Publications Ltd.
6 Bonhill Street
London EC2A 4PU
United Kingdom

SAGE Publications India Pvt. Ltd.
M-32 Market
Greater Kailash I
New Delhi 110 048 India

Printed in the United States of America

Library of Congress Cataloging-in-Publication Data

Herman, Joan L.
    Evaluator's handbook.

    (CSE program evaluation kit (2nd ed.) ; 1)
    "Center for the Study of Evaluation, University of
California, Los Angeles."
    Includes bibliographies and index.
    1. Evaluation research (Social action programs)
I. Morris, Lynn Lyons.   II. Fitz-Gibbon, Carol Taylor.
III. University of California, Los Angeles. Center for
the Study of Evaluation.   IV. Title.   V. Series:
Program evaluation kit (2nd ed.) ; 1.
H61.H455   1987   361.6'1'068   87-23386
ISBN 0-8039-3126-3 (pbk.)

SIXTH PRINTING, 1990

Contents

Acknowledgments

The preparation of this second edition of the Center for the Study of Evaluation *Program Evaluation Kit* has been a challenging task, made possible only through the combined efforts of a number of individuals.

First and foremost, Drs. Lynn Lyons Morris and Carol Taylor Fitz-Gibbon, the authors and editor of the original Kit. Together, they authored all eight of the original volumes, an enormous undertaking that required incredible knowledge, dedication, persistence, and painstaking effort. Lynn also worked relentlessly as editor of the entire set. Having struggled through only a revision, I stand in great awe of Lynn's and Carol's enormous accomplishment. This second edition retains much of their work and obviously would not have been possible without them.

Thanks also are due to Gene V Glass, Ernie House, Michael Q. Patton, Carol Weiss, and Robert Boruch, who reviewed our plans and offered specific assistance in targeting needed revisions. The work would not have proceeded without Marvin C. Alkin, who planted the seeds for the second edition and collaborated very closely during the initial planning phases.

I would like to acknowledge especially the contribution and help of Michael Q. Patton. True to form, Michael was an excellent, utilization-focused formative evaluator for the final draft manuscript, carefully responding to our work and offering innumerable specific suggestions for its improvement. We have incorporated into the *Handbook* his framework for differentiating among kinds of evaluation studies (formative, summative, implementation, outcomes).

Many staff members at the Center for the Study of Evaluation contributed to the production of the Kit. The entire effort was supervised by Aeri Lee, able office manager at the Center. Katherine Fry, word processing expert, was able to accomplish incredible graphic feats for the *Handbook* and tirelessly labored on manuscript production and data transfer. Ruth Paysen, who was a major contributor to the production of the original Kit, also was a painstaking and dedicated proofreader for the second edition. Margie Franco, Tori Gouveia, and Katherine Lu also participated in the production effort.

Marie Freeman and Pamela Aschbacher, also from the Center, contributed their ideas, editorial skills, and endless examples. Carli Rogers, of UCLA Contracts and Grants, was both caring and careful in her negotiations for us.

At Sage Publications, thanks to Sara McCune for her encouragement and to Mitch Allen for his nudging and patience.

And at the Center for the Study of Evaluation, the project surely would not have been possible without Eva L. Baker, Director. Eva is a continuing source of encouragement, ideas, support, fun, and friendship.

—Joan L. Herman
Center for the Study of Evaluation
University of California, Los Angeles

The *Program Evaluation Kit* is a set of books intended to assist people who are conducting program evaluations. Its potential use is broad. The kit may be an aid both to experienced evaluators and to those who are encountering program evaluation for the first time. Each book contains step-by-step procedural guides to help people gather, analyze, and interpret information for almost any purpose, whether it be to survey attitudes, observe a program in action, or measure outcomes in an elaborate evaluation of a multifaceted program. Examples are drawn from educational, social service, and business settings. In addition to suggesting step-by-step procedures, the kit also explains concepts and vocabulary common to evaluation, making the kit useful for training or staff development.

Components of the Kit

The *Program Evaluation Kit* consists of the following nine books, each of which may be used independently of the others.

Volume 1. The *Evaluator's Handbook* provides an overview of evaluation activities and a directory to the rest of the kit. Chapter 1 explicates the evaluation perspective which grounds the kit and describes the role of evaluation in common phases of program development. It also discusses things to consider when trying to establish the parameters of an evaluation. Chapter 2 presents specific procedural phases for conducting formative or summative evaluations. Chapters 3, 4, and 5 contain specific guides for accomplishing three general types of studies: a formative evaluation, a standard summative evaluation, and a small experiment. The handbook concludes with a master index to topics discussed throughout the kit.

Volume 2. *How to Focus an Evaluation* provides advice about planning an evaluation, that is, deciding upon the major questions the evaluation is intended to answer, the general approach, and identifying the principal audience for the evaluation. It discusses three general elements in the focusing process: existing beliefs and expectations of clients and of the evaluator, the process of gathering information, and the process of formulating an evaluation plan. Five different perspectives on the evaluation process are presented: the experimental approach; the goal-oriented approach; the decision-focused approach; the user-oriented approach; and the responsive approach.

Volume 3. *How to Design a Program Evaluation* discusses the logic underlying the use of quantitative research designs—including the ubiquitous pretest-posttest design—and supplies step-by-step procedures for setting up and interpreting the results from experimental, quasi-experimental, and time series designs. Six designs, including some unorthodox ones, are discussed in detail. Finally, the book includes instructions about how to construct random samples.

Volume 4. *How to Use Qualitative Methods in Evaluation* explains the basic assumptions underlying qualitative procedures, suggests evaluation situations where qualitative designs are useful, and provide guidelines for designing qualitative evaluations, including how to use observational methods, how to conduct in-depth, open-ended interviews, and how to analyze qualitative data.

Volume 5. *How to Assess Program Implementation* discusses the role and importance of implementation evaluation and presents methods for designing, using, and reporting the results using assessment instruments to describe accurately how a program looks in operation. Step-by-step guides are provided for program records, observations, and self-reports.

Volume 6. *How to Measure Attitudes* will help an evaluator select or design credible instruments to measure attitudes. The book discusses problems involved in measuring attitudes, including people's sensitivity about this kind of measurement and the difficulty of establishing the reliability and validity of individual measures. It lists myriad sources of available attitude instruments and gives precise instructions for developing questionnaires, interviews, attitude rating scales, sociometric instruments, and observation schedules. Finally, it suggests how to analyze and report results from attitude measures.

Volume 7. *How to Measure Performance and Use Tests* provides an overview of a variety of approaches to measuring performance outcomes. It presents considerations in deciding what to measure and in selecting or developing instruments best suited to an evaluation's goals. Methods for ensuring validity and reliability also are discussed.

Volume 8. *How to Analyze Data* is divided into three sections, each dealing with an important function that quantitative analysis serves in evaluation: summarizing scores through measures of central tendency and variability, testing for the significance of differences found among performances of groups, and correlation. Detailed worksheets, nontechnical explanations, and practical examples accompany each statistical procedure. A discussion of meta-analysis techniques also is included.

Volume 9. *How to Communicate Evaluation Findings* is designed to help an evaluator convey to various audiences the information that has been collected during the course of the evaluation. It contains an outline of a standard evaluation report, directions for written and oral reporting, and model tables and graphs.

Kit Vocabulary

For those who have had little experience with evaluation, it might be helpful to review a few basic terms which are used repeatedly throughout the *Program Evaluation Kit*. A *program* is anything you try because you think it will have an effect. A program might be something tangible, such as a set of curriculum materials; a procedure, such as the distribution of financial aid; or an arrangement of roles and responsibilities, such as the reshuffling of administrative staff. A program might be a new kind of scheduling, for example, a four-day workweek; or it might be a series of activities designed to improve workers' attitudes about their jobs.

When you *evaluate* a program, you systematically collect information about how the program operates, about the effects it may be having and/or to answer other questions of interest. Sometimes the information collected is used to make decisions about the program—for example, how to improve it, whether to expand it, or whether to discontinue it. Sometimes evaluation information has only indirect influence on decisions. Still other times it is ignored altogether. Regardless of how it is ultimately used, program evaluation requires the collection of valid, credible information about a program in a manner that makes the information potentially useful.

Generally an evaluation has a *sponsor*. This is the individual or organization who requests the evaluation and usually pays for it. If the members of a school board request an evaluation, they are the sponsors. If a federal agency requires an evaluation, the agency is the sponsor.

Evaluations always have a variety of *stakeholders* or *audiences*—groups of people who have direct or indirect interest in an evaluation's findings. Common audiences or stakeholders for information collected during program development might consist of program planners, managers, and staff who run the program. Other stakeholder groups might be the recipients of the services or products; for example, students, patients, or customers. If the program will be expanded to additional sites, or if it is reported in widely circulated publications, then the broader scientific, educational, public service, or business community makes up an evaluation audience. In short, stakeholders or audiences are the groups that you will have to keep in mind as you conduct the evaluation. If your stakeholders share a common point of view about the program or are likely to find the same evaluation information credible, consider yourself lucky. This is not always the case. Those stakeholders who are expected to *do* something as a result of an evaluation's findings—for example, make some decision or embark on a particular action—are considered *users*.

For some evaluations, of course, the roles of evaluator, sponsor, stakeholder, and user are all played by the same people. If staff or managers decide to evaluate their own programs they will be at once the sponsors, the primary users, and the evaluators—and one of several groups of potential stakeholders. Although the Kit treats these roles as distinct, it is understood that people sometimes fill overlapping functions.

One decision that an evaluator makes affects the credibility of the evaluation for many stakeholders and users. This is the selection of an *evaluation design,* a plan determining which individuals or groups will participate in the evaluation, what types of data will be collected, and when evaluation instruments or measures will be administered and by whom. The instruments could include tests, questionnaires, observations, interviews, inspections of records, and so forth. The design provides a basis for better understanding the program and its effects. More traditional quantitative designs focus primarily on measuring program results and comparing them to a standard. Such comparisons (including comparisons with other programs) give some perspective about the magnitude of a program's effect and help the evaluator and relevant audiences determine whether it indeed is the program which brings about particular outcomes. In contrast, newer *qualitative designs* focus on describing the program in depth and on better understanding the meaning and nature of its operations and effects.

The focus of the *Program Evaluation Kit* is the collection, analysis, and reporting of valid, credible information which can have some constructive impact on program decision making.

Chapter 1
Establishing the Parameters of an Evaluation

An Evaluation Framework

The field of evaluation has evolved rapidly in the last two decades, giving rise to a number of different models of the evaluation process and an evaluator's role within it. Each of these models can be seen as arising from the evaluation requirements and interests of its time and from the application of various research paradigms to the evaluation enterprise.

Models advanced in the late 1960s and early 1970s were fueled largely by the needs of large-scale curriculum developers who needed formative information to direct their revision efforts, by those of their sponsors who wanted comparative summative information to guide funding decisions, and by federal policymakers who wanted to ensure accountability for their social reforms. These models emphasized experimental methods, standardized data collection, large samples, and the provision of scientific, technical data; they also reflected general optimism that systematic, scientific measurement procedures would deliver unequivocal evidence of program success or failure. "Hard data" (i.e., empirically based data) would, it was hoped, provide both sound information for planning more effective programs and a rational basis for educational, social service, and other policy decision making. Clear cause-effect relationships, it was assumed, could be established between programs and their outcomes, and program variables could be manipulated to reach desired effects. This first wave of models—based initially on goals and then later on decisions, issues, or problems—provided decision makers and policymakers with aggregated, standardized, and technically rigorous information about prespecified program processes and outcomes. Some accused these models, however, of being superficial and insensitive to important variations in local programs.

Following this first, quantitatively grounded wave, a second wave emerged. These models were characterized by a responsiveness to unique characteristics and processes within local settings and to issues as perceived by stakeholders. Rather than assuming that social programs were discrete and easily prespecified in terms of process and outcomes, these models acknowledged that social and other programs often are complex, amorphous mobilizations of human activities and resources that vary significantly from one locale to another, embedded in and influenced by complex political and social networks. Rare is the program, according to these model builders, which exists in hermetically sealed isolation, perfectly appropriate for scientific measurement and duplication. Their models, as a result, stressed the importance of naturalistic, qualitative methods for understanding the means of operation and the effects of programs. While providing in-depth understanding of unique program configurations—understanding that is critical to program improvement aims—these models unfortunately lacked easy or credible ways of aggregating or generalizing findings across sites, a distinct disadvantage for accountability and/or higher-level decision making.

Concurrent with the growth of responsive models came renewed attention to the utility of evaluation findings. Spurred by federal and state mandates in the late 1960s and 1970s, thousands of evaluations were conducted across the country. Unfortunately many, if not most, of these evaluations did not have the expected impact; researchers questioned whether these evaluations had any impact at all. Continuing to believe in the potential contribution of their work to social policy, planning, and practice, some evaluators became concerned about how to ensure that their findings were used, not simply filed. These model builders stressed the importance of sociopolitical and other factors beyond technical quality which were critical to an effective (i.e., useful) evaluation process.

The literature of evaluation, in short, has been marked by various models which have served to conceptualize the field and to draw boundaries on the role of the evaluator. General trends in emphasis have been described above, and brief descriptions of some of the more prominent models appear in Table 1. (Most of these are explicated further in the *How to Focus an Evaluation*, Volume 2 of the kit; those who plan to spend considerable time working as an evaluator also may want use the references shown in Table 1 and the readings listed in the "For Further Reading" section to get a more detailed view of what evaluators have said about their craft.) It is worth

TABLE 1

Some Models of Program Evaluation

Model	Emphasis	Selected References
Goal-oriented evaluation	Evaluation should assess student progress and the effectiveness of educational innovations.	Bloom, B. S., Hastings, J. T., & Madaus, G. F. (1971). *Handbook on formative and summative evaluation of student learning.* New York: McGraw-Hill. Popham, W. J. (1975). *Educational evaluation.* Englewood Cliffs, NJ: Prentice-Hall.
Decision-oriented evaluation	Evaluation should facilitate intelligent judgments by decision makers	Stufflebeam, D. L. (Ed.). (1971). *Educational evaluation and decision-making.* Itasca, IL: F. E. Peacock. Alkin, M. C. (1969). Evaluation theory development. *Evaluation Comment, 2,* 2-7.
Responsive evaluation	Evaluation should depict program processes and the value perspectives of key people.	Stake, R. E., et al. (1975). *Evaluating the arts in education: A responsive approach.* Columbus, OH: Charles E. Merril.
Evaluation research	Evaluation should focus on explaining effects, identifying causes of effects, and generating generalizations about program effectiveness.	Campbell, D. (1969). Reforms as experiments. *American Psychologist, 24,* 409-429. Rossi, A., & Freeman, H. E. (1985). *Evaluation: A systematic approach* (3rd ed.). Newbury Park, CA: Sage.
Goal-free evaluation	Evaluation should assess program effects based on criteria apart from the program's own conceptual framework, especially on the extent to which real client needs are met.	Scriven, M. (1974). Pros and cons about goal-free evaluation. In W. J. Popham (Ed.), *Evaluation in education: Current applications.* Berkeley, CA: McCutchan.
Advocacy-adversary evaluation	Evaluation should derive from the argumentation of contrasting points of view.	Wolf, R. L. (1975). Trial by jury: A new evaluation method. *Phi Delta Kappan* (November).
Utilization-oriented evaluation	Evaluation should be structured to maximize the utilization of its findings by specific stakeholders and users.	Patton, M. Q. (1986). *Utilization-focused evaluation.* Newbury Park, CA: Sage. Alkin, M., Daillak, R., & White, P. (1979). *Using evaluations.* Newbury Park, CA: Sage.

stressing that while these models are distinguished by emphasis, they are *not* mutually exclusive.

What model does this *Program Evaluation Kit* espouse? Rather than advocating a single model, this kit has drawn its prescriptions about how to conduct evaluations from most of the models in Table 1. Each model is appropriate to particular sets of interests and circumstances and has its own strengths and weaknesses. Since the kit's purpose is to help you plan and conduct the best possible evaluation for your situation, its advice is eclectic and focuses not only on how to accomplish the technical requirements of an evaluation but also on how to structure your evaluation to facilitate the use and impact of its findings. The advice is grounded, however, in a specific perspective on both the role and the limits of evaluation in policy and in the improvement of practice.

Conceptual Framework of the
Center for the Study of Evaluation (CSE)

The conceptual framework on which the *Program Evaluation Kit* rests recognizes the complexities of evaluation and proposes a comprehensive and eclectic approach to solve them. (See Baker & Herman, 1985, for an expanded discussion of this model.) Underlying the framework is a continuing belief that evaluation can play an integral role in improving program operations and can contribute to enlightened policymaking at federal, state, local, agency, and corporate levels. Well-conceived, well-designed, and thoughtfully analyzed evaluations can provide valuable insights into how programs are operating, the extent to which they are serving their intended beneficiaries, their strengths and weaknesses, their cost-effectiveness, and potentially productive directions for the future. By providing relevant information for decision making, evaluation can help to set priorities, guide the allocation of resources, facilitate the modification and refinement of program structures and activities, and signal the need for redeployment of personnel and resources. And it can serve such functions for policymakers, administrators, and implementers at all levels, from the individual program provider, to program managers at various levels, through the highest-level policymakers, helping them to assess and improve the quality of their programs and policies.

A simplified picture of the role of evaluation in improving program quality and policy is displayed in Figure 1. The model displays the interactions among the formulation and implementation of program policies and practices and the assessment and evaluation of their quality. At the simplest level, policies are formulated to guide program practice; but because program operations are subject to policy interpretation and to local site and individual adaptation, practices do not precisely mirror their guiding policies. Policies and practices then combine to produce the actual quality of a program (or the quality

of an organization's operations). Through evaluation, that quality is assessed, a process which can be either qualitative or quantitative but which in either case can address only partially the total quality of program effort and its effects. Following assessment, evaluation judgments are reached about how well policies and practices are working. These judgments may be strongly influenced by explicit goals, objectives, and standards, but they also develop from a wide range of other values as well. Depending on the judgment, decisions may be reached to continue or alter existing policies and/or to continue, eliminate, expand, or modify current operating practices. The model is arrayed in a circle to indicate that the process is neither discrete nor linear. The display also indicates that the process operates within important social, political, and organizational contexts which exert and are subject to significant influence.

The point of entry in the model just described corresponds roughly to a traditional view of the role of evaluation in program development, but other points of entry and other orders clearly are possible. Taken from another point, for example, substantiated or unsubstantiated evaluations of quality (e.g., vague feelings of "things aren't working very well here") can lead to assessments which identify needs for new interventions in policy and practice—the needs assessment role of evaluation. Those new interventions may be subsequently assessed and evaluated, and become the subject of continued or modified actions.

What differentiates this model from more traditional ones is a recognition of the role of both implicit and explicit realities and of the importance of formal and informal sources of information in decision making. A number of points are worth noting briefly. First, the model recognizes that formal policies and plans provide only general guidelines and only loosely control actual practices. Second, policies and practices are dependent on formal and informal assessments and understandings of how a program is operating and its effects. These assessments can capture only a part of a program's quality and provide only rough, imperfect estimates of reality. Third, the model recognizes that judgments and evaluations about quality in reality are based on the integration of various sources of information against general values and expectations, only some of which are represented in explicit program goals, objectives, and standards. Fourth, the model highlights the effect of contextual factors on the evaluation of programs and on the actions (or inaction) resulting from them. Changing policy expectations, resources and other constraints, as well as social, organizational, political, and demographic factors significantly affect the process and impact of evaluation. *Evaluation, in short, is an endeavor which is partly social, partly political, and only partly technical.*

The *Program Evaluation Kit* reflects the need for a flexible approach that considers the complex environment

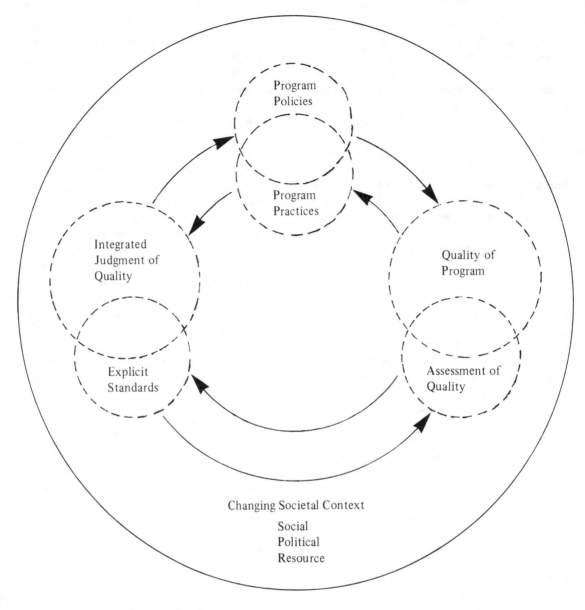

Figure 1. The quality improvement process (QIP) model

in which a program exists as well as the purpose and context of its evaluation. Evaluators must be aware of the decision-making context within which the evaluation is to occur. They must consider the perceptions and expectations of various audiences, the developmental phase of the program under investigation, as well as the technical issue of which methodology to use in gathering data.

Evaluation During the Life of a Program

While recognizing that the development of policy and programs (and evaluation's role in that development) is neither simple nor linear, it nonetheless is useful to think about hypothetical phases during the life of a program when evaluation and the credible information it creates

can make a contribution. Four such phases are described below. Clearly these phases are not inviolate or clearly separate; they quite often overlap, and some programs skip certain phases entirely. Thinking about the phases, however, can help an evaluator to conceptualize the stakeholders, functions, and decisions an evaluation is to serve.

Program initiation

Early in the development of a new policy or program, sponsors, managers, and planners consider the goals they hope to accomplish through program activities and identify the needs and/or problems that a program is supposed to redress. Formally or informally, every program, in fact, goes through some kind of needs assessment—even though it may not be obvious whose needs are being defined or that the process is very rigorous. In some cases the needs are simply assumed, and planners proceed to structure activities accordingly. At other times, the sponsor or funding agency more or less declares a need by making money available for programs aimed at general goals. Sometimes, however, a systematic data-gathering effort is conducted to verify that perceived needs actually exist, to rank their importance, and/or to identify specific underlying problems. If a school program is intended as a response to community needs, for example, an evaluator may help to articulate those needs by gathering information from and about parents, teachers, students, and a sample of the broader community. Similarly in trying to help structure a program to increase staff morale, an evaluator may observe closely and survey employees, their supervisors, experts, and others in order to uncover the source of the morale problem and its potential solution. While such formal needs assessments often try to gather input from a broad range of sources, sometimes a more restricted approach is preferable—for example, where problems are very specialized or highly technical. In such cases, an evaluator might solicit only experts' views.

The point is that new programs or changes in existing programs are often initiated in response to critical needs, in order to achieve (at least someone's) high priority goals or to solve existing problems. Evaluation information in this context can help program designers focus their efforts.

Program planning

A second phase in the life of a program is its planning. Ideally, a program is designed or revised to meet the high priority goals as established by a needs assessment or as identified in a formative or summative evaluation. At times the need to reach certain goals will prompt planners to design a new program from scratch, putting together materials, activities, and administrative arrangements that have not been tried before. Other situations will require that they purchase and install, or moderately adapt, an already existing program. Both situations qualify as program planning: something that has not occurred previously in the setting is created for the purpose of meeting desired goals. During this phase, controlled pilot testing and market testing can be used to assess the effectiveness and feasibility of alternative methods of addressing primary needs and goals. While it is desirable to establish plans for conducting evaluations during this planning phase, practice rarely meets this ideal.

Program implementation

A third phase may occur as the program or changes in it are being installed. Suppose, for example, that urban planners want to try out a new management information system. Purchases are made, boxes delivered, and training planned. This will be the first year of the new system. Ideally, the program's sponsors should give the new system a chance to iron out mistakes, solve problems, and reach the point where it is running smoothly before they judge its effectiveness. All the time a program is in this implementation stage, subject to trial and error, the staff is trying to operationalize it suitably and adapt it as necessary to work in their particular setting. Evaluations during this phase need to provide formative information, that is, information which describes how the program is operating and contributes to ways to improve it. *Formative evaluation* can take many forms: special surveys of program services, ethnographic studies, interview studies, or analyses of administrative records to determine how the program actually operates; progress testing to monitor its effects; or management studies to see how administrative arrangements may be functioning. In these formative cases, the evaluator may work very closely with the program and staff and report both formally and informally about findings as they emerge.

Program accountability

When a program has become established with a permanent budget and an organizational niche, it might be time to question its overall effectiveness and impact—and perhaps to make judgments about whether or not to continue the program, whether or not to expand it, and whether or not to recommend the program for use in other locales. During this phase, an evaluation may be termed *summative* and is generally of most direct concern to program policymakers.

Ideally, because the summative evaluator represents the interests of the sponsor and the broader community, he or she should try *not* to interfere with the program. The summative evaluator's function is *not* to work with the staff and suggest improvements while the program is running, but rather to collect data and write a summary report showing what the program looks like, what has been achieved, and what implications and recommendations may be derived for improving future efforts and/or informing public policy. Many recommend that for the sake of credibility, the summative evaluator should not get involved with the program beyond data collection—making measurements, conducting observations, interviewing, and so on—and should remain detached and independent from the program. Such independence supposedly enables an evaluator to be free to report negative findings, a crucial ingredient for credibility. Such detachment, however, is easier said than done and may not always be desirable from an evaluation use perspective.

Political realities make such an idealized summative evaluation a rarity in practice. Why? Discussions of the difficulty of producing objective summative evaluations point to four causes:

(1) Regardless of who commissions the evaluation, directives to evaluators often require that they serve an ambiguous formative/summative function. Many evaluators are asked to work on improvement of a program and to write a summary report. Evaluators, then, may be scrutinizing programs in which they have personal stakes or have established collegial relationships, and objectivity may be compromised.

(2) Many funders request that the project staff hire its own evaluator. Because evaluators in this instance are essentially in the employ of the local staff and may wish to receive commissions to evaluate in the future, they may be loath to report negative findings. Evaluations conducted under these circumstances understandably may err in the direction of praise.

(3) Few sponsors' funding programs take the hard-line, consumer advocacy point-of-view expressed in CSE's definition of summative evaluation. The prestige of a foundation or a department of the government, after all, comes from funding *effective* programs. Negative results may be seen as serving no one's benefit.

(4) The process of planning and conducting a useful evaluation often requires rapport, trust, and frequent interaction with program administrators. The element of trust, in fact, may figure prominently in the quality of one's data. (The validity of interview data, for example, depends on candid responses.) Yet the processes leading to such trust and rapport may color an evaluator's perspective.

Some of these problems are confounded by recent trends toward hiring evaluators as permanent members of an organization's staff. These individuals often are an adjunct to management, working to increase organizational efficiency and effectiveness on a regular basis. Sometimes their role may be formative, working closely with management and program planners to see how programs and operations may be improved. At other times, they may be asked to provide a more summative perspective, assessing whether program outcomes are worth the cost. While this trend shows an admirable institution of the evaluation function and acknowledges the importance of evaluation in sound management practice, it carries with it some difficult built-in conflicts. Consider, for instance, the situation of the evaluator assigned to training programs for a large utility company. Over the last year, this evaluator has worked closely with the same program designers to develop a large array of personnel training programs. The evaluator currently is working with designers and instructors to devise an approach that will help identify the strengths and weaknesses of each session, carefully building in their ownership and trust and utilizing data collection procedures that require their close cooperation. Management has just told the evaluator they want to use the results of the evaluation to decide whether they should continue their in-house training operations.

In short, divided loyalties, personal relationships, and professional stakes and allegiances can give rise to significant dilemmas. Evaluators, regardless of where or how they are employed, need to find viable ways to maintain integrity, objectivity, and an appropriate sense of differentiation.

Conceptualizing Your Evaluation

"We'd better have an evaluation of Program X," someone could decide, and then appoint you to carry out that decision. Proceed with this caution:

> Your first act in response to this assignment should be to find out what evaluation means in this instance. Find out what is expected. What purpose is to be served? What information will the evaluation be expected to provide? Does the sponsor or another user want more information than you can possibly provide? Do they want definitive statements that you will not be able to make? Do they want you to take on an impartial or advocate role toward the program that you cannot in good conscience assume?

Failure to reach a common understanding about the exact nature of the evaluation could lead to wasted money and effort, frustration, and acrimony if sponsors feel they did not get what they expected. Step one in any evaluation is to negotiate!

Immediately after accepting the assignment, try to get a clear picture of what you will be expected to do. Your conceptualization will have six major considerations, each negotiated with the sponsor and the primary users or stakeholders:

(1) A decision about what people really want when they say they want an evaluation.

(2) Identification of what the audiences will accept as credible information.

(3) Choice of a reporting style. This may include the extent to which you report quantitative or qualitative information, whether you will write technical reports, brief notes, or confer with the staff, and the timing of important reports.

(4) Determination of a general technical approach based upon information and credibility needs.

(5) A decision of what to measure and/or gather information about.

(6) Delineation of what you can accomplish within the constraints of the evaluation's budget and political situation.

Each of these six considerations will be discussed in more detail below.

Determining What People Really Want When They Say They Want an Evaluation

The sponsor who commissions the investigation and/or the primary users it is intended to serve may have in mind any number of activities that could be called evaluation. What kind—or, more likely, kinds—of investigation will best serve their needs is a function of the primary purposes of their inquiry and of the program areas that are of most interest to them. Are the users most interested in forward planning, in improving an ongoing or developing program, or in making judgments about program success? Are their questions aimed at the way the program operates and/or on its outcomes? The matrix displayed in Figure 2 provides a heuristic for thinking about the different kinds of studies that are possible and the emphases which may be appropriate for yours.

Helping your primary sponsor or users to articulate the principal purpose(s) the study is to serve a good starting point in identifying what people really want to know. The matrix in Figure 2 lists three purposes that sponsors typically have in mind when they request an evaluation:

- To conduct a needs assessment to identify goals, products, problems, or conditions which should be addressed in future program planning;
- To conduct a formative evaluation to help program planners, managers, and/or staff improve a developing or ongoing program;
- To conduct a summative evaluation to help the sponsor or others in authority decide the extent to which a program is successful and what should be its ultimate fate.

How will the findings be put to use? Who are the *primary* intended users? At what general stage is the development of the program in the evaluation taking place? Answers to these questions will help you to identify the main purpose(s) your sponsor(s) has in mind. This purpose, in turn, affects the specific questions your study should address, your relative emphasis on program implementation and outcomes, and the level of program detail at which you seek to provide answers. (Chapter 2 expands on the differences which typically accompany the different evaluation purposes.)

The concept of *relative emphasis* on program implementation and on outcomes is an important one. Almost all evaluations, regardless of purpose, will want to give at least some attention to both program areas. Knowing that program goals were reached without knowing whether the program in fact was implemented is insufficient to determine whether the program was successful (perhaps the goals would have been reached anyway). Similarly, looking solely at how program components are being implemented without any consideration of their impact makes it difficult to determine whether and how they might be productively changed. While it is usually the case that summative evaluations emphasize questions dealing with attainment of program goals, objectives, and other outcomes, and formative evaluations generally emphasize questions related to how the program is operating, exceptions are not uncommon. Sometimes in summative evaluation, for example, it is not possible—because of the limits of available technology or because of the resource or other constraints on the evaluation—to assess accurately whether program objectives have been achieved, and therefore the study may focus on implementation questions to document whether the program actually was implemented as designed. As another example, whether the program can be implemented as designed and as funded may be the crucial policy question driving a summative study.

Determining what people want when they say they want an evaluation, thus, is a complex endeavor, requiring frequent interactions with the sponsor and primary users early in the study and the simultaneous consideration of the purposes they have in mind and the program areas they are most interested in having studied. The charts on pages 16 to 18 briefly describe the types of investigations which may be conducted in support of these purposes and interest areas. Each briefly summarizes the types of questions which the sponsor, primary users, and evaluator might typically consider, the general activities that could be expected to occur, and the decisions that might be affected. The type of study(ies) you conduct, remember, will represent a unique combination of purpose(s) and interest area(s). For example, your users may be interested primarily in an implementation study aimed at formative purposes, in a needs assessment to identify the outcomes which a subsequent program should address, in a summative evaluation focusing on program objectives, or any (one or several) of a number of possible combinations. Note that the recommendations for conducting formative and summative evaluations in subsequent chapters of this handbook encompass the activities required for almost all of the possibilities.

Needs Assessment

Many requests for "evaluation" actually require a needs assessment. By probing, the evaluator might discover that the aim of the evaluation is neither to decide between continuing or dropping a program—summative evaluation—nor to help develop detailed, specific activities to improve a program—formative evaluation. Rather, the sponsor wants to discover weaknesses or problem areas in the current situation which can eventually be remedied or to project future conditions to which the program will need to adjust. Watch particularly for this substitution of "evaluation" for "needs assessment" when the program to be evaluated is large and complexly organized, with many goals, components, and staff roles, and where there is general dissatisfaction or uneasiness about program effectiveness: "Our nursing program needs evaluating" or "We need to evaluate our food services." Notice especially that a needs assessment frequently is used to make public implicit goals and/or to re-examine and critique existing goals.

| | Program Area of Most Interest | |
Purpose of Inquiry	Outcomes	Implementation/ Process
Needs Assessment		
Formative Evaluation		
Summative Evaluation		

NOTE: We are indebted to Michael Patton for suggesting this conceptualization.

Figure 2

Decisions and actions likely to follow a needs assessment

The decisions following a needs assessment usually involve allocation of money and effort to meet high priority needs. The activities that should follow are planning of programs or revisions of them—in terms of education, organization, whatever—addressed to the identified needs. Note that needs assessment can be rather similar to formative evaluation but formally differs in the typical size or scope of the program under investigation, and more particularly in the fact that formative evaluators often follow up the identification of weaknesses. They may work with the staff to attempt improvements during the course of the evaluation. In a needs assessment, on the other hand, the survey of needs is itself the end product.

Formative Evaluation

Formative evaluation encompasses the thousand-and-one jobs connected with providing information to the staff to get the program running smoothly. It might even include conducting a needs assessment. Certainly it will involve some attention to monitoring program implementation and achievement of goals. In order to improve a program, it will be necessary to understand how well a program is moving toward its objectives so that changes can be made in the program's components. Formative evaluation is time-consuming because it requires becoming familiar with multiple aspects of a program and providing program personnel with information and insights to help them improve it. Before launching into formative evaluation, make sure that there actually is a chance of making changes for improvement; if no such possibility exists, formative evaluation is not appropriate.

Decisions and actions likely to follow a formative evaluation

As a result of formative evaluation, revisions are made in the staffing, activities, organization, and other materials of the program. These adjustments may be made throughout the formative evaluation process.

CHART 1 NEEDS ASSESSMENT

(Also called an Organizational Review)

Questions on the minds of the sponsors and audiences

What needs attention?

What should our program(s) try to accomplish?

Where are we failing?

Kinds of questions the evaluator might pose

What are the goals of the organization or community?

Is there agreement on the goals from all groups?

To what extent are these goals being met?

What do clients perceive they need? What problems are they experiencing?

What do staff perceive they need? What problems are they experiencing?

How effective is the organization in addressing problems perceived by clients?

What are the areas in which the organization is most seriously failing to achieve goals?

Where does it need to plan special programs or revise old programs?

Kit components of greatest relevance

How To Focus an Evaluation

How To Measure Performance and Use Tests

How To Measure Attitudes

How To Assess Program Implementation

How To Use Qualitative Methods in Evaluation

Summative Evaluation

The goal of summative evaluation is to collect and to present information needed for summary statements and judgments about the program and its value. The evaluator should try to provide a basis against which to compare the program's accomplishments. One might contrast the program's effects and costs with those produced by an alternative program with the same goals. In situations where such a comparison is not possible, participants' performance might be compared with a group receiving no such program at all. The standard for comparison might come from the norms of achievement tests or from a comparison of program results with the goals identified by the program designers or the community at large.

In some instances, summative evaluation is not appropriate. A summary statement should not be written, for instance, about a program that has not been in existence long enough to be fully developed. The more a program

CHART 2   FORMATIVE EVALUATION

Questions on the minds of sponsors and audiences

How can the program be improved?

How can it become more efficient or effective?

Kinds of questions the evaluator might pose

What are the program's goals and objectives?

What are the program's most important characteristics—materials, staffing, activities, administrative arrangements?

How are the program activities supposed to lead to attainment of the objectives?

Are the program's important characteristics being implemented?

Are program components contributing to achievement of the objectives?

Which activities or combination best accomplish each objective?

What adjustments in the program might lead to better attainment of the objectives?

What adjustments in program management and support (staff development, incentives, etc.) are needed?

Is the program or some aspects of it better suited to certain types of participants?

What problems are there and how can they be solved?

What measures and designs could be recommended for use during summative evaluation of the program?

Kit components of greatest relevance

All of them.

CHART 3   SUMMATIVE EVALUATION

(Also called Outcome Evaluation, Consumer Testing, Evaluation Research)

Questions on the minds of sponsors and audiences

Is Program X worth continuing or expanding?

How effective is it?

What conclusions can be made about the effects of Program X or its various components?

What does Program X look like and accomplish?

Kinds of questions the evaluator might pose

What are the goals and objectives of Program X?

What are Program X's most important characteristics, activities, services, staffing, and administrative arrangements?

Why should these particular activities reach its goals?

Did the planned program occur?

Does the program lead to goal achievement?

What programs are available as alternatives to Program X?

How effective is Program X? In comparison with alternative programs?

Is the program differentially effective with particular types of participants and/or in particular locales?

How costly is the program?

Kit components of greatest relevance

All of them

has clear and measurable goals and consistent replicable materials, organization, and activities, the more suited it is for a summative evaluation.

Decisions and actions likely to follow a summative evaluation

Decision makers may use information from summative evaluations to help them decide whether to continue or to discontinue a program or whether and/or how to expand or reduce it.

Implementation Studies

Program implementation studies focus on the activities, services, materials, staffing, and administrative arrangements that compose a program and how those entities operate. Users want a description of who is doing what in

Program X, or of how a requirement has been interpreted by program planners and developers across sites. Often they want to use the information formatively —for example, to uncover where things are going well, where they may need modification, and what kinds of changes are likely to help.

Other times the information is used summatively. Sponsors and other users may be willing to judge or make decisions about the program on the basis of whether or not they think the activities occurring are valuable in themselves or probably will be effective in achieving other goals. This is particularly true when the program is designed to reflect a philosophy or theory of how particular kinds of organizations should be run in order to achieve long-term goals that cannot be immediately measured, or when the question of whether the program *can* be implemented as designed and funded is the central policy issue.

CHART 4 IMPLEMENTATION STUDY

(Also called a Program Documentation or Evaluation of Program Process)

Questions on the minds of the sponsors and audiences

What is happening in the Program X?

To what extent has the program been implemented as designed?

How much does the program vary from site to site?

Kinds of questions the evaluator might pose

What are the critical activities, staffing, and administrative arrangements, etc. in the program?

How many participants and staff are taking part?

When? How often? Where?

Is the program running as planned?

What is a typical schedule of activities and/or of services?

How are time, money, and personnel allocated?

What activities do participants in the program become involved in?

How does the program vary from one site to another?

Kit component of greatest relevance

How To Assess Program Implementation

How To Use Qualitative Methods

CHART 5 OUTCOME STUDIES

(Also called Objectives-Based Evaluation)

Questions on the minds of sponsors and audiences

To what extent is Program X meeting its goals?

Is there steady progress toward the attainment of objectives?

Kinds of questions the evaluator might pose

What are the goals of the program?

How can they be measured or otherwise assessed?

What do measures show about the degree of goal attainment?

What other outcomes are associated with the program?

What objectives and subobjectives are essential to the attainment of program goals?

What gaps exist in these attainment of objectives or subobjectives?

Kit components of greatest relevance

How To Focus an Evaluation

How To Measure Performance and Use Tests

How To Measure Attitudes

How To Use Qualitative Methods

Outcome Studies

Outcome studies examine the extent to which a program's highest priority goals are and are not being achieved. Some of these goals might be affective, such as satisfaction with the program; others might be cognitive, such as knowledge or skill gain; still others may be performance or behavior-based, such as abstention from drugs or a reduction in child abuse. Program goals are usually stated in terms of participant (student, client, etc.), staff, or others' outcomes. While explicit program goals are of primary emphasis, the vigilant evaluator also needs to attend to potential unanticipated or unstated outcomes, both positive and negative.

It should be noted that clarification and measurement of goals often helps planners and staff to better focus their activities on goals and make revisions in areas where goals are failing to be achieved.

What Will Be Accepted as Credible?

In addition to finding out what your audiences want to know, you will need to discover what they will accept as credible information. The credibility of the evaluation will, of course, be influenced by your own credibility, a judgment that will be based on your competence as well as your personal style. For some, your perceived competence in technical skills may be most important; for others your sensitivity in reporting may be paramount. For others still, your background in program subject matter may be the primary consideration. In any event, your evaluation will be more useful and its various users and audiences less skeptical if they are confident you know what you are doing. A skilled evaluator therefore needs strong interpersonal skills and the ability to nurture trust and rapport with various users and audiences.

Your users' willingness to accept without question what you report will be based on other criteria as well. For one thing, they will take account of your allegiances. To be credible, evaluators must be perceived as free to find fault—whether or not they do. This means that you should not be constrained by friendship, professional relations, or the desire to receive future evaluation jobs. In addition, audiences will believe what the evaluator reports to the extent that they see that person as representing themselves. Unfortunately, these requirements may work at cross purposes. A program staff, for instance, may be suspicious of a formative evaluator who will write a summary report at year's end to the funding agency. The agency, on the other hand, will read the report suspiciously if it suspects that formative work has put an evaluator on the staff's or program designers' "side." Because of these credibility problems, evaluators with ambiguous formative-summative job descriptions have to carefully negotiate their roles and expertly develop rapport and trust with the various audiences. Under these circumstances, the ideal posture may be to be perceived as a colleague who is able to understand the perspectives and problems of program staff but who is willing to be constructively critical, and who will collect and impartially analyze information in order to make honest and helpful recommendations.

Another determiner of how seriously users listen to your results is their faith in the methods you use for gathering information. Methods of data-gathering include the evaluation design; the instruments administered; the people selected for testing, questioning, or observation; and the times at which data (measurements, observations, etc.) are gathered. Sometimes the methods you use will be largely predetermined by legal or funding requirements. At other times the specific methods you select will depend on whether you and your users favor quantitative approaches or qualitative approaches, or something in between.

When you choose a general approach, select methods of gathering information and designs, or construct a sampling plan, remember this: you cannot count on your audience to accept as credible the same sorts of evidence that you consider most acceptable. People are usually skeptical, in fact, of arguments they do not understand. You might have noticed that when reports filled with complicated data analyses are presented, people stay quiet until a few experts have given their opinions. Then everyone discusses the opinions of the experts.

Unless your users are very sophisticated and expect complex analyses, consider keeping your design, data-gathering, and analyses simple and straightforward. Think of yourself as a surrogate, delegated to gather and digest information that your audience would gather on its own if it were able. Keep a few representative users of the evaluation in mind, and ask youself periodically, "Will Mr. Carson see the value in collecting this data or in doing this analysis?" A good way to find out, of course, is to ask Mr. Carson.

Remember, as well, that the general public tends to place more faith in opinions and anecdotes than do researchers—at least usually. If you plan to collect a large amount of "hard" data you will have to educate people about what it means. And you may want to supplement the numbers with some anecdotal information to help your audience understand their meaning.

Deciding on Reporting Requirements and Style

Why worry about reporting when you're conceptualizing your evaluation project? First, because each formal report requires time to both write and produce, reporting can have important implications for the project budget, particularly if different reports are to be produced to meet the needs of different audiences. Formal reports, too, are only part of what is required to help ensure a useful evaluation project: reporting, both formal and informal, should be an ongoing process during the life of an evaluation, not just an end-of-project product.

A second reason for considering reporting requirements early is their influence on the methodology and impact of the evaluation. How reports are perceived by their potential audiences, the credibility of the evidence presented, and the persuasiveness of findings and conclusions are dependent not only on what is presented but on how it is presented as well. What kinds of reports are desired? Preferred *reporting style* is applicable here. It refers to the relative weight a report gives to quantitative and to qualitative data and the degree of formality with which the report is delivered. Do the primary users, for example, prefer evidence in the form of tables of means and percentages, in the form of charts and graphs, and/or in the form of characteristic anecdotes? Are written reports, oral briefings, or high-tech media shows desired? Such preferences need to be articulated and negotiated early in the planning process. (The kit book, *How to Communicate Evaluation Findings*, should be of help to you as you negotiate a reporting strategy.)

Determining the General Evaluation Approach

Part of what determines the credibility of an evaluation, as mentioned above, is the credibility of the technical approach—the credibility of the design, methods, measures, and so on that are utilized for answering the questions of interest in the evaluation. How do you choose an appropriate technical approach? The answer lies in the interplay between the evaluator's predispositions, client preferences, and most important the information needs of the evaluation. (*How to Focus an Evaluation* further describes this interplay.)

Quantitative Approaches

You are probably aware that technical approaches are often dichotomized into two general categories: quantitative approaches and qualitative approaches. Quantitative approaches have been most prevalent historically in evaluation studies, particularly in evaluation studies intended to measure program effects. Quantitative approaches are concerned primarily with measuring a finite number of prespecified outcomes, with judging effects, with attributing cause by comparing the results of such measurements in various programs of interest, and with generalizing the results of the measurements and the results of any comparisons to the population as a whole. The emphasis is on measuring, summarizing, aggregating, and comparing measurements, and on deriving meaning from quantitative analyses. (Quantitative approaches also may be used in rating, classifying, and quantifying particular predefined aspects of program implementation.) Such approaches often utilize experimental designs, frequently employ control groups, and are particularly important when program effectiveness is the primary evaluation issue.

The Importance of Design and Control Groups in Quantitative Approaches

Why are designs and control groups so important? You probably already know a bit about design—that it involves assignment of students, clients, or staff to programs and to comparison or control groups. The purpose of this discussion is to present you with the logic underlying the need for good design in evaluations where you want to show that there is a relationship between program activities and outcomes.

First consider the common before-and-after design. In the typical situation, a new program has been instituted and an evaluation planned. The evaluator administers a pretest at the beginning of the program and at the end of the program a posttest, as in the following examples:

- A new district-wide mathematics program is evaluated. The California Achievement Test is administered in September and again in May.
- A new halfway house program has set itself the goal of decreasing recidivism in its juvenile clients. The evaluator observes and records the number of arrests and of convictions of its clients at the beginning of the year and then again at the end of the year.
- An objective of a corporate reorganization project is to increase staff morale and productivity. Staff fills in a questionnaire at the beginning of the year and then again at the end of the year; productivity indices likewise are computed at the beginning and end of the year.

Differences on the pre- and posttests are then scrutinized to determine whether the program did what it was supposed to do. This is where the before-and-after design leaves the evaluation vulnerable to challenge. It fails to answer two important questions:

(1) How good are the results? Could they have been better? Would they have been the same if the program had not been carried out?
(2) Was it the program that brought about these results or was it something else?

Consider the following situation. A new math program has been put into effect in the Lincoln District. Ms. Pryor,

the superintendent, wants to assess the quality of the program by examining students' grade equivalent scores from a standardized math test given in September and then again in May. She notes that the sixth grade average was 5.4 in September and 6.5 in May. She attempts to judge the value of the new math program based on this pretest-posttest information.

Results on State Math Test—6th Grades

Math Program	Sept. Pretest (G.E.)	May Posttest (G.E.)
Sunnydale Learning Associates	5.4	6.5

The Lincoln students in the example have shown a considerable gain in math from pretest to posttest—1.1 grade equivalent points. On the other hand, they are still not performing at grade level. Therefore Ms. Pryor must ask herself, "How good are these results?" The answer depends, of course, on the children and the conditions in the school and home. For some groups, this would represent great progress; for others, it would indicate serious difficulties in the program.

How can Ms. Pryor find out what progress she should expect from her sixth graders? The pretest tells her something: the sixth-graders were six months behind in September, and they ended up only four months behind in May. Perhaps without the new program they would have ended up five months behind, or perhaps they would have done better with the old program! In order to know what difference the program made, she needs to know how the students would have scored without the program.

Ms. Pryor has another problem in interpreting her results. She cannot even show that the gains she did get on the posttest were brought about by the new program. Perhaps there were other changes that occurred in the school or among the students this year—a drop in class size, or a larger number of parents volunteering to tutor, or the miraculous absence of "difficult" children who demanded teacher time and distracted the class. Many influences might cause the learning situation to alter from year to year.

Ms. Pryor could have ruled out most of these explanations of her results by using a control group. First, two randomly formed groups would have been assigned at the beginning of the year to either the new math program or to another semester of the old one (or to another alternative program). Before the program began, both groups would have been pretested. At the end of the year, the groups would be posttested using the same math test. Because the two groups were initially equivalent, the scores of the control group would show how the new program students would have scored if they had not received the new program:

Program	Pretest	Posttest
Sunnydale (x)	5.4	6.5
Old Program (Control Group)	5.4	6.1

But was it the new program that brought about the improvement, or was it some other factor? Using a true control group design, Ms. Pryor can discount the influence of other factors as long as these factors have probably also affected the control group. If, for instance, some students had had an enriched nursery school program that got them off to a good start in math, the random assignment should have spread these students fairly evenly between the two groups. If more parents were helping in the school, this should have benefitted both groups equally. If this year's sixth grade was generally quieter, with fewer difficult children, this should have affected both the experimental and control groups equally. Ms. Pryor does not even have to know what all the factors might have been. By randomly assigning the two groups, the influence of various factors affecting the math achievement of the two groups is likely to be equalized. Then differences observed in outcomes can be attributed to the one factor that has been made deliberately different: the math program.

Though much maligned as impractical, the true control group design produces such credible and interpretable results that it should at least be considered an ideal to be approximated when evaluation studies are planned.[1] The design is valuable because it provides a comparative basis from which to examine the results of the program in question. It helps to rule out the challenges of potential skeptics that good attitudes or improved achievement were brought about by factors other than the program.

Nonetheless, it is not always easy to convince people that random assignment and experimentation are good things; and of course you must make design decisions that are consistent with the constraints of your situation. Consider using a design in the administration of each measurement instrument you will use. Consider a randomized design first. If this is not possible, then look for a non-equivalent control group—people as much like the program group as possible but who will receive no program or a different program. Or try to use a time-series design as a basis for comparison: find relevant data about the former performance of program groups or of past groups in the same setting. Only if none of these designs is possible should you abandon using a design. An evaluation that can say, "Compared to such-and-such, this is what the program poduced" is more interpretable than one like Ms. Pryor's that simply reports scores in a vacuum. (*How to Design a Program Evaluation* provides more detail on this subject.)

Qualitative Approaches Also Can Be Important

While experimental design and control groups have traditionally been advocated in evaluation studies, qualitative methods have been given increasing attention in recent years. In contrast to the traditional deductive approach used in quantitative approaches, qualitative methods are inductive. The researcher or evaluator strives to describe and understand the program or particular aspects of it as a whole. Rather than entering the study with a pre-existing set of expectations or a prespecified classification system for examining or measuring program outcomes (and/or processes), the evaluator tries to understand the meaning of a program and its outcomes from the participants' perspectives. The emphasis is on detailed description and on in-depth understanding as it emerges from direct contact and experience with the program and its participants. Using more naturalistic methods of gathering data, qualitative techniques rely on observations, interviews, case studies, and other means of fieldwork. (*How to Use Qualitative Methods in Evaluation*, Volume 4 of the kit, provides more detail about qualitative approaches and their rationale.)

Traditionally, qualitative and quantitative approaches have been seen as diametrically opposed, and many evaluators still strongly espouse one approach or the other. More recently, however, this dichotomy is beginning to soften, and more and more evaluators are beginning to see the merits of combining both approaches in response to differing requirements within an evaluation and in response to different evaluation contexts. For example, if the purpose of an evaluation is to determine program effectiveness and the program and its outcomes are well defined, then a quantitative approach may well be appropriate. If, on the other hand, the purpose of an evaluation is to determine program effectiveness but the program and its outcomes are poorly defined, an evaluator might start with a qualitative approach to identify critical program features and potential outcomes and then employ a quantitative approach to assess their attainment. To take another, different example, suppose the purpose of an evaluation is program improvement, and more particularly the identification of promising practices that might be adopted in a number of program sites. An evaluator might use a quantitative approach to identify sites which were particularly successful in achieving program outcomes and then use a qualitative approach to understand how the successful sites were different from those with less success and to identify those practices which appear related to program success.

There are numerous compelling reasons, then, why an evaluator might want to incorporate qualitative approaches into his study. *How to Use Qualitative Methods in Evaluation* expands on a number of them, including the following situations:

- when a program emphasizes individualized outcomes
- when decision makers are interested in understanding the dynamics of program processes and program implementation
- when program staff want detailed descriptive information to help them improve the program
- when there is concern for the nuances of program quality
- when decision makers/funders who are too busy for site visits want an evaluator to be their surrogate eyes and ears
- when unobtrusive observation is needed
- when goals of a program are vague, general, or nonspecific
- when unanticipated outcomes or unexpected side effects are a concern
- where there is a need to add depth, detail, and meaning to empirical findings

There is no single correct approach to all evaluation problems. The message is this: some will need a quantitative approach; some will need a qualitative approach; probably most will benefit from a combination of the two.

Deciding What to Measure or Observe

Having decided on a general approach, an evaluator might decide to measure, observe, and/or analyze an infinite number of things: smiles per second, math achievement, time schedules, district innovativeness, sick days taken, self-concept, leadership, morale, and on and on. The options are many and varied, and an evaluator, in concert with the sponsor and primary users, will need to make some tough decisions.

The program's objectives, your role, and your users' motives will help you to make gross decisions about what to look at. In making such decisions, you will want to consider five general aspects of a program that might be examined as part of your evaluation:

- context characteristics
- participant characteristics
- characteristics of or processes in program implementation
- program outcomes
- program costs

Looking at all five aspects will help to ensure comprehensive evidence that can document the effects of a program or of one of its subcomponents and/or that can help to improve it. Within and across each category, however, be prepared to face inevitable tradeoffs between the depth and breadth of information you are able to collect.

Context Characteristics

Programs take place within a setting or context—a framework of constraints within which a program must operate. They include a complex network of sociopolitical factors that influence almost all programs (e.g., power, leadership, communications) as well as program specific factors, such as class size, time frame within which the program must operate, budget, and specific incentives. It is especially important to get accurate information about aspects of the context that you suspect might affect how a program operates and its success. If, for example, you suspect that programs like the one you are evaluating might be effective under one style of governance but not under another kind, you may want to assess leadership style at the various sites to explore that possibility.

Participant Characteristics

Personal characteristics include such things as age, sex, socioeconomic status, language dominance, ability, attendance record, attitudes, and background/experience. It may sometimes be important to see if a program shows different effects with different groups of clients. For example, if teachers say the least well-behaved students seem to like the program but the best-behaved students do not like it, you may want to collect information about "well-behavedness" prior to the program and examine your results to detect whether these different reactions did indeed occur. Similarly, if you suspect that a rehabilitation center may be differentially effective with first-time versus repeat offenders, you would want to be sure to collect information on participants' prior history.

Characteristics of Program Implementation

Program characteristics are the program's principal activities, services, processes, materials, staffing, and administrative arrangements. Program characteristics are the things people do to try to achieve the program's goals. You will almost certainly need to describe these; but since most programs have so many facets, you will have to narrow your focus to those that seem most important to funders, program planners, or staff, or to those perceived as most in need of attention. In summative evaluations, these will usually be the processes and characteristics that distinguish the program from other similar ones. In formative evaluations, these will usually be those aspects of the program which are most problematic.

Program Outcomes

In most evaluations, you will want to measure or observe the extent to which goals have been achieved. You must make sure, however, that all the program's important objectives have been articulated. Be alert to detecting unspoken goals such as the one buried in this comment: "I could see how much the audience enjoyed the program. This alone convinced me the program was good." At least in the eyes of this speaker enjoyment was a program goal, or a highly valued outcome, whether or not this was so stated in program plans.

Be alert also to unanticipated outcomes—both positive and negative—that may be associated with a program. Imagine, for example, a reading program that succeeds in its goal of increasing student achievement but in the process snuffs out students' desire to read for pleasure. Or a new incentive program that achieves its goal of increasing productivity for existing products and services but has adverse affects on the initiative and creativity necessary to ensure successful new ventures.

You also need to consider both long- and short-range outcomes. Some of the most important hoped for outcomes may be so long-range that only a study of many years' duration could definitely establish that they had occurred. This would be the case, for example, with goals such as "increased job satisfaction in adult life" or "a lifelong love of books." Nonetheless, it is possible and desirable to find proximate, short-term indicators that may predict significant long-term outcomes.

An evaluator in general should focus the evaluation on announced goals, but would be well advised to include also the wishes of the program's larger constituency—for example, the community—in formulating the yardsticks against which the program will be assessed.

Program Costs

Evaluation data about program outcomes are supposed to support rational planning, decision making, and judgments about whether to continue, expand, or cancel particular programs. But knowledge about the effects of the program provides only a part of the information needed to make decisions about resource allocations. Such decisions hinge not only on effectiveness in terms of outcomes, but also on required resources and on the relative cost- effectiveness of competing alternatives. For example, suppose an innovative program to combat absenteeism has been found to be 20% more effective than the traditional program, clearly a very positive finding. Yet a policymaker's response to that finding may vary considerably depending on whether the costs of the two programs are roughly comparable, widely disparate, and/or whether wider implementation of the program would require policymakers to use all their discretionary resources.

As a result, evaluators often will want to gather data about program costs. These include obvious costs, such as staff time, materials, equipment, facilities, as well as indirect, opportunity, and other hidden costs.

Beyond these general guidelines, decisions about exactly what information to collect will be situation specific. Every program has distinctive goals; and every situation makes available unique kinds of data. Though there is no simple way to make these decisions, some more specific rules of thumb are offered in the next chapter.

Delineating What You Can Accomplish Within Budgetary and Other Constraints

You, your clients, and primary users probably will be interested in many more questions and issues than can possibly be covered in a single evaluation. Financial limitations and political climate are important constraints on an evaluation which always affect the scope and depth of its investigations. The amount of time evaluators can devote, limitations on *who, where,* and *when* they can measure or observe, and constraints on *what* they can ask all determine the ultimate breadth and quality of an evaluation.

The amount of time an evaluator can devote to the project is dependent on the available budget. Available time combined with other available resources, in turn, significantly influences methodological choices. Site visits, for example, are costly in terms of staff time as well as travel. Special outcome measures, as another example, require substantial staff time for development, pilot-testing, and analysis. Assessing more rather than fewer program participants, as a third example, has significant cost implications. Rarely are abundant resources available for an evaluation, and the evaluator often must juggle artfully to maintain a reasonable balance between the demands of scientific rigor and credibility and those of the budget. (Sometimes such a balance is just not possible and clients need to be informed accordingly.)

But financial resources represent only a part of the constraints on any evaluation. Some writers have expressed pessimism about the usefulness of evaluation results because of the overriding social and political motives of the people who are supposed to use them for making decisions. Ross and Cronbach (1976) describe the situation this way:

> Far from supplying facts and figures to an economic man, the evaluator is furnishing arms to a combatant in a war with fluid lines of battle and transient alliances; whoever can use the evaluators to gain an inch of terrain can be expected to do so . . . The commissioning of an evaluation . . . is rarely the product of the inquiring scientific spirit; more often it is the expression of political forces.

The political situation could hamper an evaluation in several ways. For one, it might place constraints on data collection that make accurate description of the program impossible. The sponsor could, for instance, restrict the choice of sites for data collection, regulate the use of certain designs or tests, or withhold key information. Politics could, as well, cause the evaluator's report to be ignored or its results to be misinterpreted in support of a particular point of view. Responding to any of these situations will depend on vigilance in each unique case. Remember that your major responsibility as an evaluator is to collect good information wherever possible.

How might an evaluator alleviate some of these political forces? First, remember the old adage "Forewarned is forearmed" and be aware of the political forces at work in your situation. Second, try to neutralize the influence of competing agendas by drawing the representatives of powerful constituencies into the evaluation process. Identify the relevant decision makers and information users and work with them to identify program needs and to focus the evaluation. On this point, *The Standards for Evaluations of Educational Programs, Projects, and Materials* developed by the Joint Committee on Standards for Educational Evaluation (1981) states,

> The evaluation should be planned and conducted with anticipation of the different positions of various interest groups, so that their cooperation may be obtained, and so that possible attempts by any of these groups to curtail evaluation operations or to bias or misapply the results can be averted or counteracted.

Because of the acknowledged political nature of the evaluation process and the political climate in which it is conducted and used, it is imperative that you as the evaluator examine the circumstances of every evaluation situation and decide whether conforming to the press of the political context will violate your own ethics. It could turn out that the data that audiences want, or the kinds of reports required, do not suit your own talents or standards, or the standards of the profession.

The point is that all evaluations operate within a set of constraints—financial, political, and other—that influence both what an evaluation can accomplish and its potential impact. The evaluator needs to be aware of these various constraints and to plan accordingly for the most effective evaluation possible.

There's No Easy Answer

What should be clear after reading this chapter is that evaluation is a complicated endeavor, and that there is no single approach that will solve all problems. Professional evaluators in education have struggled with the issue of what constitutes a good evaluation. Unable to issue a simple formula or easy recipe, the Joint Committee on Standards for Educational Evaluation has issued *Standards for Evaluations of Educational Programs, Projects, and Materials* (1981). The standards reflect general agreement about the principles which should be observed in evaluating programs and represent a set of criteria against which quality can be judged. The 30 standards are grouped to define four essential attributes of a good evaluation:

- *Utility standards* seek to ensure that an evaluation will serve the practical information needs of given audiences. These standards include audience identification, evaluator credibility, information scope and selection, valuational interpretation, report clarity, report dissemination, report timeliness, and evaluation impact.
- *Feasibility standards* seek to ensure that an evaluation will be realistic, prudent, diplomatic, and frugal. These include practical procedures, political viability, and cost-effectiveness.

- *Propriety standards* seek to ensure that an evaluation will be conducted legally, ethically, and with due regard for the welfare of those involved in the evaluation, as well as those affected by its results. These include formal obligation, conflict of interest, full and frank disclosure, public's right to know, rights of human subjects, human interactions, balanced reporting, and fiscal responsibility.
- *Accuracy standards* seek to ensure that an evaluation will use technically adequate information about the features of the object being studied that determine its worth or merit. These include object identification, context analysis, described purposes and procedures, defensible information sources, valid measurement, reliable measurement, systematic data control, analysis of quantitative information, analysis of qualitative information, justified conclusions, and objective reporting.

A good evaluation, in short, is useful to its audience, practical to implement, conducted ethically, and technically accurate.

Note

1. Actually, true control group designs have been used in evaluation of many educational and social programs. A list of 141 of them, with references, is contained in Boruch (1974).

References

Baker, E., & Herman, J. (1985). Educational evaluation: emergent needs for research. *Evaluation Comment, 7*(2), 1-12.

Boruch, R. F. (1974). Bibliography: Illustrative randomized field experiments for program planning and evaluation. *Evaluation, 2*(1), 83-87.

Joint Committee on Standards for Educational Evaluation. (1981). *The standards for evaluations of educational programs, projects, and materials.* NY: McGraw-Hill.

Ross, L., & Cronbach, L. J. (1976). Review of the *Handbook of Evaluation Research. Educational Researcher, 5*(10), 9-19.

For Further Reading

Alkin, M. C. (1969). Evaluation theory development. *Evaluation Comment, 2,* 2-7.

Alkin, M., Daillak, R., & White, P. (1979). *Using evaluations.* Newbury Park, CA: Sage.

Attkisson, C. C., Hargreaves, W. A., Horowitz, M. J., & Sorenson, J. E. (1978). *Evaluation of human service programs.* New York: Academic Press.

Baker, E. L., & Herman, J. L. (1985). Educational evaluation: Emergent needs for research. *Evaluation Comment, 7,* 2.

Bennett, C. A., & Lumsdaine, A. A. (Eds.). (1975). *Evaluation and Experiment.* New York: Academic Press.

Bloom, B. S., Hastings, J. T., & Madaus, G. F. (1971). *Handbook on formative and summative evaluation of student learning.* New York: McGraw-Hill.

Boruch, R. F. (1974). Bibliography: Illustrative randomized field experiments for program planning and evaluation. *Evaluation, 2*(1), 83-87.

Boruch, R. F., Sweeney, A. J., & Soderstrom, E. J. (1978). Randomized field experiments for program planning, development, and evaluation: An illustrative bibliography. *Evaluation Quarterly, 2,* 655-695.

Bryk, A. (Ed.). (1983). *Stakeholder-based evaluation: New directions for program evaluation* (Vol. 17). San Francisco: Jossey-Bass.

Campbell, D. T. (1972). Reforms as experiments. In C. H. Weiss (Ed.), *Evaluating action programs: Reading in social action and education.* Boston: Allyn & Bacon.

Catterall, J. (Ed.). (1985). *Economic evaluations of public programs: New directions for program evaluation.* San Francisco: Jossey-Bass.

Cook, T. D., & Reichardt, C. S. (Eds.). (1979). *Qualitative and quantitative methods in evaluation research.* Newbury Park, CA: Sage.

Cronbach, L. J. (1982). *Designing evaluations of educational and social programs.* San Francisco: Jossey-Bass.

Cronbach, L. J., et al. (1980). *Toward reform of program evaluations.* San Francisco: Jossey-Bass.

Glass, G. V (1976). *Evaluation studies review annual* (Vol. 1). Newbury Park, CA: Sage.

Guba, E. G., & Lincoln, Y. S. (1981). *Effective evaluation: Improving the usefulness of evaluation results through responsive and naturalistic approaches.* San Francisco: Jossey-Bass.

Guttentag, M., & Struening, E. L. (1975). *Handbook of evaluation research* (Vols. 1-2). Newbury Park, CA: Sage.

House, E. R. (1980). *Evaluating with validity.* Newbury Park, CA: Sage.

Joint Committee on Standards for Educational Evaluation. (1981). *Standards for evaluations of educational programs, projects, and materials.* New York: McGraw-Hill.

Levin, H. M. (1983). *Cost effectiveness: A primer.* Newbury Park, CA: Sage.

Lincoln, Y. S., & Guba, E. G. (1985). *Naturalistic inquiry.* Newbury Park, CA: Sage.

Madaus, G. F., Scriven, M., & Stufflebeam, D. L. (1983). *Evaluation models: Viewpoints on educational and human services evaluation.* Boston: Kluwer-Nijhoff.

Moos, R. (1975). *Evaluating correctional and community settings.* New York: John Wiley.

Patton, M. Q. (1986). *Utilization-focused evaluation* (2nd ed.). Newbury Park, CA: Sage.

Popham, W. J. (1975). *Educational evaluation.* Englewood Cliffs, NJ: Prentice-Hall.

Pressman, J. L., & Wildavsky, A. (1984). *Implementation.* Berkeley: University of California Press.

Reichardt, C. S., & Cook, T. D. (1979). Beyond qualitative versus quantitative methods. In T. Cook & C. S. Reichardt (Eds.) *Qualitative and quantitative methods.* Newbury Park, CA: Sage.

Rossi, P. H., & Freeman, H. E. (1985). *Evaluation: A systematic approach* (3rd ed.). Newbury Park, CA: Sage.

Scriven, M. (1967). The methodology of evaluation. In American Educational Research Association, *Perspectives of curriculum evaluation.* Chicago: Rand McNally.

Stake, R. E. (1967). The countenance of educational evaluation. *Teachers College Record, 68,* 523-540.

Scriven, M. (1974). Pros and cons about goal-free evaluation. In W. J. Popham (Ed.), *Evaluation in education: Current applications.* Berkeley: McCutchan.

Stake, R. E., et al. (1975). *Evaluating the arts in education: A responsive approach.* Columbus, OH: Charles E. Merrill.

Stufflebeam, D. L., Foley, W. J., Gephart, W. J., Guba, E. G., Hammond, R. L., Merriman, H. O., & Provus, M. M. (1971). *Educational evaluation and decision-making.* Itasca, IL: Peacock.

Wolf, R. L. (1975). Trial by jury: A new evaluation method. *Phi Delta Kappan, 57*(3) 185-218.

Chapter 2

How to Play the Role of the Formative or Summative Evaluator

The chapters which follow provide guidance on how to conduct two kinds of evaluation studies: formative evaluations, which focus on providing information to planners and implementers on how to improve and refine a developing or ongoing program; and summative evaluations, which seek to assess the overall quality and impact of mature programs for purposes of accountability and policymaking. While it is easy to make clear distinctions between the two on paper, reality often is more muddled. Rare indeed is the program that is so mature and that functions so flawlessly that recommendations for improvement are of no interest! Less rare is the program that is mature, even aged, in years of program operation but in great need of formative services to prod it toward effectiveness. Relatively rare, too, is the evaluation where program impact is ignored and where findings will not be used to document program effectiveness for funders and other policymakers. In short, definitions are easy, but rare is an evaluation that does not have both formative and summative aspects. Particularly in time of scarce resources (in other words, almost always), policymakers, program planners, and managers often will want a single evaluation to serve a multiplicity of purposes—given a choice they will want to garner sound data they can use to support future fund raising (or funds maintenance) and at the same time data that can contribute to more effective programming.

Why, then, have we chosen to treat these two aspects of evaluation separately? From our vantage point, formative and summative evaluation represent two ends of a continuum. At the extremes, the two types are quite different: from the evaluator who functions as a member of the program planning team, interested solely in how to modify, augment, or streamline a program in order to make it work better, to the evaluator working in the service of policymakers, interested only in scientifically documenting program effects. Although most users of this kit will find themselves functioning at some point between these two ends, they probably will be balanced closer to one end than the other. Understanding the contrasts may help them better fulfill their functions. Table 2 lists some of these contrasts.

Despite these differences in audiences, timing, em-

TABLE 2

Comparative Emphases in Formative Versus Summative Evaluation

	Formative	Summative
Primary audience	program developers/ program managers program implementers	policymakers interested publics funders
Primary emphasis in data collection	clarification of goals the nature of program process/implementation clarification of problems in implementation and in progress on outcomes micro-level analyses of implementation and outcomes	documentation of outcomes documentation of implementation macro-level analyses of implementation and outcomes
Primary role of program developers and implementers	collaborators	data providers
Primary role of evaluator	interactive	independent
Typical methodology	qualitative and quantitative, with more emphasis on former	quantitative, sometimes enriched with qualitative
Frequency of data collection	ongoing monitoring	limited
Primary reporting mechanisms	discussion/meetings informal interaction	formal reports
Reporting frequency	frequent throughout	at conclusion
Emphasis in reporting	relations among process elements—micro level relations among context and process relation between process and outcome implications for program practices and specific changes in operations	macro-relations context process outcome implications for policy, administrative controls, and management
Requirements for credibility	understanding of program rapport with developers/ implementors advocacy/trust	scientific rigor impartiality

phases, and the nature of the relationship between the evaluator and the program, the *Program Evaluation Kit* uses a common set of general phases to organize its step-by-step guides for conducting formative and summative evaluations. The nature of the tasks which constitute each phase, of course, will vary depending on whether an evaluation is more formative or more summative. Salient commonalities and differences among these phases are described in the remainder of this chapter. The phases described here are:

Phase A: Set the Boundaries of the Evaluation
Phase B: Select Appropriate Evaluation Methods
Phase C: Collect and Analyze Information
Phase D: Report Findings

You might think of each phase as a set of information-gathering activities culminating in one or more meetings where decisions are made about the next information-gathering cycle. Although it would be logical to perform the tasks subsumed under each phase in the sequence presented above, you may well find yourself working at two or more phases simultaneously or cycling back through them again and again. If you are a formative evaluator, this will be particularly the case with Phases C and D; you might collect, report, and discuss implementation and progress data many times during the course of the evaluation. If you are a summative evaluator, on the other hand, you may well need to cycle back and forth between focusing activities (Phase A) and methods selection (Phase B) in order to reach firm agreement on what the evaluation is to accomplish and with what budget. In either case, meetings with primary users are likely to involve tasks in more than one phase.

Phase A: Set the Boundaries of the Evaluation

As soon as you have hung up the telephone, having spoken with someone requesting an evaluation, you must begin to establish the boundaries of the evaluation. It could be that the person asked you outright to help with project improvement (formative evaluation) or perhaps you were asked to provide information to determine whether or not Program X should be funded next year. More likely, however, your caller will not have been so directive. In any case, your first job as either a summative or a formative evaluator will be to decipher the nature of the study you are being asked to complete (formative, summative, or a combination) and to delineate the scope of the evaluation by sketching out the issues or questions your evaluation will address and the tasks you intend to accomplish. If your charge is primarily summative, you would negotiate this scope with program sponsors or primary decision makers; if, on the other hand, your charge is primarily formative, you probably would want to draw in program managers and staff very early during the process. This negotiation will result in a plan describing what you will do as an evaluator as well as what the staff and others will do to help you gather information and to act upon what you report. These are some key questions at this stage of your work: Who wants the evaluation done? Why is it being requested? What are the most important users and audiences for the findings? What is to be done as a result of the evaluation? What is the nature of the program to be evaluated? Refer to *How to Focus an Evaluation*, Volume 2 of the *Program Evaluation Kit*, for suggestions for managing this planning process.

Research the Program

Even before your first meeting with your potential client, you should find out as much as possible about the program, a process that will continue intensely throughout the planning and negotiation process. A recommended first activity is to contact someone who is familiar with this or similar programs (if you are not such a person). In addition to sharing basic information, such a person may be able to help you anticipate problems in the program or its evaluation, critical features of the socio-political context, and/or potential pitfalls in developing good relationships with managers, staff, and others.

By all means ask for documents related to funding and development or adoption of the program. These documents might include an RFP (request for proposals) issued by the funding source when it first offered money for such programs, the program plan or proposal, and program descriptions written for other reasons such as public relations. Use these documents to form an initial understanding of what the program is supposed to look like, what its goals might be, and particularly what shape the evaluation might take.

In addition, it may be worth your while to check quickly the literature of the field to see what, if anything, has recently been written about programs like the one in question or about specific components that the program includes. You may even find earlier evaluations of this or similar programs. Doing such advance homework will enable you to be both knowledgeable and sensitive in your first meeting with study sponsors and able to use that meeting productively to probe and clarify the intended scope of your study.

Encourage Trust, Cooperation, and Ownership

Your first meeting with study sponsors will help to set the climate and the working relationships for your study. A good and useful evaluation depends upon sharing information and upon cultivating a constituency of potential users who believe that the evaluation addresses prime issues of concern and has produced valid, reliable and credible results—in other words, a constituency who will trust the findings.

One way to encourage such trust is to involve the primary potential users in planning for the evaluation and to facilitate their ownership of the study. Solicit from them the significant goals and effects of the program as they view them (anticipated and unanticipated), key program players, key features of program implementation, problems that are likely or have occurred, and so forth. Consider also provisions for their review of the evaluation plans, including the nature and content of instrumentation, the timing of data collection, and the nature of reporting.

Who are the key evaluation constituencies who need to be cultivated? An important problem during the focusing process will be identifying who these constituencies are. The emphasis will vary depending on the kind of evaluation you are being asked to conduct; but at the simplest level, pay attention to constituencies who are intended to be the primary users of the results of your evaluation and to those constituencies who must view the results as credible for the findings to be used. For most summative evaluations, the study funders and/or primary program policymakers (legislators, boards, foundations, federal agencies, top-level managers) represent the primary constituencies, although program staff, clients, the public, and others may need to be consulted to ensure that your study is fairly focused on program realities and is viewed as credible.

If, on the other hand, your role is primarily formative, your key potential users will be those charged with enacting the program and with whom you will collaborate on program changes—program managers, staff, and other key actors. If your evaluation has been commissioned by the program staff itself, establishing trust with them will be easier than if the evaluation has been externally mandated. The formative evaluator will need to convince the staff that his or her primary objective is to help them discover how to optimize program implementation and outcomes and that the information will not be used against the staff. Whenever it is possible, you might also want to guarantee that information shared for the purpose of internal program review and improvement will be kept confidential. "Actions speak louder than words" is a telling adage in this situation. An important way to gain the confidence and trust of program personnel is to make yourself useful from the very beginning, efficiently and sensitively collecting information they need and would like to have and helping them to use the information to improve their program.

If you play a dual role with regard to formative and summative evaluation, your position is more difficult. You will need to work very hard to alleviate the concerns of a potentially defensive staff and emphasize that their open communication with you is their best guarantee that your summative report will fairly represent their views. The latter is a critically important point when your role is primarily summative. You need to be clear that your role is to provide an unbiased report of program accomplishments, a report that will give equitable attention to staff perspectives.

Articulate Your Understanding of the Program

While mutual trust must be worked out gradually, some of the more practical aspects of your role and the scope of your work can be negotiated earlier. Key to your role will be the nature of the program to be evaluated, and you will want to articulate your understanding in a program description very early on.

A program description sets forth a written list, or at least an outline of such a list, of the principal goals and objectives of a program, the central activities and materials which are supposed to accomplish those goals and objectives, and the rationale which describes the relationships between these intended means and ends. If your role is principally summative, your description may be accomplished fairly easily: you need describe only agreed upon end-of-program goals and objectives and specific contours of major activities and components. Be aware, though, that you will need to prepare two descriptions if you are planning a comparative approach to your study: a description of the program you are evaluating and one of the program to which it is being compared. On the other hand, the description task may be far more difficult and, in fact, may constitute the major part of your evaluation effort if you are serving as a formative evaluator, particularly if the program is still in the early stages of development or only weakly specified. If you are in the latter situation, do not expect to formulate a complete program description at this point; instead your task is to identify gaps and fuzzy areas needing sustained attention during Phase B. Helping program managers and staff to articulate a detailed plan of what they are trying to accomplish, how they intend to accomplish it, and the rationale undergirding their efforts often can serve in and of itself to facilitate program improvement; be careful, however, not to underestimate the time, effort, and delicacy required to reach consensus.

Whether your role is formative or summative, you will need to identify and acquire an understanding of program goals and the activities and arrangements that are intended to facilitate them.

Identify program goals. There are three basic sources of information about program goals:

- the program plan, proposal, and other official documents;
- interviews and informal dialogues with program staff; and
- naturalistic observation-based inferences about program emphases.

Although you should get a glimpse of how the program will function from documents such as the program's proposal or the program plan, often these consist of exhaustive lists of documented needs that the program should meet, a page or two on objectives, and a description of the program's staffing and budget. A good description of what people taking part in the program do or have done to them often cannot be found.

Be aware also that official documents represent only formal statements of program intentions. These may be outdated, incomplete, erroneous, or unrealistic. Written descriptions of categorically funded programs are particularly misleading: their objectives often reflect only politically minded rhetoric. Canned programs, or sets of published program materials, are another source of official objectives. But be careful here as well. While adoption of a particular program may reflect a philosophy shared between program planners and staff and the developer of the materials, it also is possible that the staff running this particular program consciously or unconsciously possess a different set of goals or that the program will only use certain components of purchased materials.

Because of the problems associated with goals listed in official documents, document review is never enough. You will need to obtain and/or verify goal information from discussions which probe the motives of the program decision makers, staff, and others and from observations of the program. Simply asking staff members and others their perceptions of program objectives will often elicit a recitation of documented goals, clichés, or socially desirable answers. Asking your informants for scenarios of what you might see or expect to see at program sites is sometimes more productive. These scenarios can be followed by questions about the particular effects that are expected to result from the activities described. You may also find it easy to elicit statements from staff members about which aspects of the program are free to vary and which are not; this information too can shed light on the program's aims and rationale. Be sensitive to inconsistencies in perceptions and particularly to disagreements which seem to be a function of group membership. For example, the public perceives one set of goals, staff another, and program administrators still another.

Record the program's rationale. Careful examination of the rationale underlying the program goes hand in hand with efforts to understand the program. The rationale on which any program is based, sometimes called its theory of action or its process model, is simply a statement of why this program—a particular set of implemented activities, services, materials, and/or administrative arrangements—is expected to produce the desired outcomes. Sometimes the relationship between methods and goals is transparent; but other times, particularly with innovative programs, the credibility of the program requires that the staff explain and justify program methods and approaches.

Example. A team of teachers from four high schools in a large metropolitan area planned a work-study program. The purpose of the program was to teach career savvy. The teachers defined this as "knowledge about what it takes to be successful in one's chosen field of endeavor." The district assigned a consultant to the project, Anna

Smith, whose job it was to help teachers iron out administrative details involved with coordinating student placement. Ms. Smith had also been told to serve in whatever formative evaluation capacity seemed necessary.

Having discovered that the teachers did not write a proposal for the program, she asked that they meet with her so that she could write a short document describing the program's major goals and outlining at least the skeleton of the program. At this meeting teachers described the basic program. Students would choose from among a set of communitywide jobs made available at minimum pay by various professional and business firms. The students would work as office clerks, salespersons, receptionists; they might be called on to make deliveries and do odd jobs.

Instantly Ms. Smith saw that the program was without a clear rationale. "What makes you think," she asked, "that students will gain an understanding of the important skills involved in carrying on a career as a result of their taking on menial jobs?" The staff had to admit that the program as planned did not guarantee that students would learn about the duties of people in different careers or about prerequisite skills for success. Together with Ms. Smith, they restructured the program as follows:

- They added an observation-and-conversation component to ensure that sponsoring professionals and businesspeople would commit some time to describing their personal career histories and would allow the students to observe the course of their workday.
- Students would be required to keep journals and read about the career of interest.

As a formative evaluator, look for potential problems. As a formative evaluator, you will want to be alert to potential snags in the program plan or its rationale. A mismatch may arise, for example, when staff grossly underestimate the time needed for the program to produce its effects or try to accomplish too many objectives or objectives that are too ambitious for a project of moderate duration.

The production and/or refinement of the written statement during a formative evaluation provides a good opportunity for planners to describe concretely the program they envision. Because a formative evaluator may have the job of writing an official statement for the staff, you will be able to ask difficult questions without implying any criticism. In describing goals and activities, and especially in exploring the logic of the connection between them, the program managers or staff may encounter contradictions, uncertainties, and conflicts that you will have to handle with tact, patience, and persistence. Their sense of ease with you in your evaluator role will be reflected in the degree of candor with which they participate in these discussions. Interviews with program staff and firsthand observations might need to replace group discussions as your primary source of information if staff members find it too hard to articulate goals, strategies, and rationale in group settings.

If, in fact, there is a total lack of consensus concerning what the program is about, you may find it necessary to do a retrospective needs assessment with the staff. Such a needs assessment might result in lists of goal priorities and preferred approaches, determined by polling the needs and preferences of important stakeholder groups and by analyzing existing or newly collected data about how well these needs are being filled by the current program (e.g., statistical data about student achievement, nutritional needs, crime statistics, health data). If you find little consensus about your program, consider planning a needs assessment during Phase B.

Elicit Information from Key Constituencies to Determine the Limits of Your Evaluation

Understanding the nature of the program to be evaluated is one key problem in planning an evaluation. Your role as an evaluator is grounded in that understanding and negotiated to fit within the specific needs and interests of each evaluation context. While your formal negotiations will be conducted with the principal sponsor for the evaluation, you probably will want to confer with key user constituencies before you reach final decisions.

For formative studies. As indicated above, an evaluation done for formative purposes requires a close working relationship with the staff as you jointly determine the most appropriate course for your efforts. If you arrive early during program development, you may find that the staff needs help in identifying program goals and in developing and/or choosing related materials, activities, and so on; this is help you will plan to provide during Phase B. Even after the program has begun, they may still be planning. And even very late in the program history, they may be grappling with some important planning issues, such as "Things aren't working so well, what's the problem? How can we make things better?" Regardless of the age of the program or the state of program development when you begin, you should help the staff outline what they consider to be the principal characteristics of their program and its primary goals, highlighting those which they consider to be fixed and those which they consider *changeable enough to be the focus of formative evaluation.*

If your evaluation is planned to stimulate program improvement, a clear picture of staff and planners' *commitment to change* is an important framing issue, that is, try to find out the extent to which they really intend to use the information you collect to make modifications in the program. Though neither you nor they will be able to anticipate beforehand precisely what actions will follow on the information you report, you should get some idea of the extent to which managers, staff, and planners are willing to alter the program. If they are unwilling, your evaluation efforts may be fruitless.

In general, laying the groundwork for a formative evaluation means asking the planners and staff such questions as:

- Which parts of the program do you consider its most distinctive characteristics, those that make it unique among programs of its kind?
- Which aspects of the program do you think wield greatest influence in producing the attitudes or achievement the program is supposed to bring about?
- What components would you like the program to have which it does not contain currently? Might we try some of these on a temporary basis?
- Which parts of the program as it looks currently are most troublesome, most controversial, or most in need of vigilant attention?
- On what are you most and least willing, or constrained, to spend additional money? Would you be willing or could you, for instance, purchase another computer program? Can you hire additional personnel or consultants?
- Where would you be most agreeable to cutbacks? Can you, for instance, remove personnel? If expensive equipment were found to be ineffective, would you eliminate it? Which materials and other program components would you be willing to delete? Would you be willing to scrap the program as it currently looks and start over?
- How much administrative or staff reorganization will the situation tolerate? Can you change people's roles? Can you add to staff, say, by bringing in volunteers? Can you move people from location to location permanently or temporarily? Can you reassign individuals to different programs or groups?
- How much change will you tolerate in the program beyond its current state? Would you be willing to delete, add, or alter the program's objectives? To what extent would you be willing to change books, materials, and other program components? Are you willing to redesign the total approach or particular parts of it?

The reason behind asking these questions is twofold: to help you better understand the program and to uncover particularly malleable aspects of the program. By asking these hard questions early, you also find out about the staff's commitment to change. A dedicated staff that has worked diligently to plan a program will likely have in mind a point beyond which it will not go in making modifications. You should locate that point, and choose the program features you will monitor accordingly.

Try to help the staff outline areas of the program where modifications are likely to be either necessary or possible; then they can begin to delineate the parts of the program whose effectiveness should be scrutinized. This, in turn, will suggest the kinds of information they will need. If the program is based on canned procedures or materials which will simply be installed, or on materials not expressly designed for the type of program in question, then what you can change will be restricted. In this case, you should focus on how best to make materials or procedures fit the context.

In the case where a wholly new program is being developed, you will want to identify the most promising sorts of modifications that can be made within existing budget limitations. You may find it most useful to concentrate on helping the staff select from among several alternatives the most popular or effective form the program can take.

Example. KDKC, an educational television station serving a large city, received a contract from the federal government to produce 13 segments of a series about intercultural understanding directed at middle grade students. The objective of the series would be to promote appreciation of diverse cultures by depicting life in the home countries of the major cultural groups composing the population of the United States.

The producers of the series set out at once to assemble the programs based on the format of popular primary grade programs: the central characters living in a culturally diverse neighborhood converse with each other about their respective backgrounds. These conversations lead into vignettes—filmed and animated—depicting life and culture in different countries. Some members of the production staff, however, suggested that a program format suitable for the primary grades may "bomb" with older students. "How do we know," they asked, "what interests 10- and 11-year-olds?" They suggested two formats which might be more effective: a fast action adventure spy story with documentary interludes and a dramatic program focusing on teenage students traveling in different countries.

To test these intriguing notions, the producer called on Dr. Schwartz, a professor of child development. Dr. Schwartz, however, had to admit that he was not sure what would most interest middle grade students either. Since the federal grant included funds for planning, Dr. Schwartz suggested that the producer assemble three pilot shows presenting basically the same knowledge via each of the three major formats being considered and then show these to students in the target age group, assessing what they learned and their enjoyment. The producer liked the idea of letting an experiment determine the form of the programs and agreed to allow Dr. Schwartz to conduct the studies, serving as a formative evaluator.

A final consideration in uncovering staff loyalties and attitudes is their commitment to a particular philosophy. If they are adopting a canned program, their philosophy probably motivated their choice. Staff members developing a program from scratch may also subscribe to a single motivating philosophy. However, you may find it poorly articulated or even not clearly evidenced in the program. In this case, you can create a basis for future decision making by helping the staff to clarify and put into practice what their philosophy says.

For summative studies. While summative evaluators are not so much interested in potential areas of program change, they are interested in focusing the evaluation on key features and outcomes of the program and on the policy questions which may underlie the program. As indicated above, summative evaluators are well advised to confer with key stakeholders in the evaluation before reaching final decisions about the focus for their study. Among the questions to pose to these stakeholders as well as to the study sponsor are the following:

- What are the most important outcomes of the program, including planned, serendipitous, and unanticipated?
- Which parts of the program do you consider its most distinctive characteristics, those that make it unique among programs of its kind?
- Which aspects of the program do you think wield greatest influence in producing program outcomes?
- What are the most critical organizational and administrative aspects of the program?
- What characteristics does the typical client possess? Does the program serve a variety of clients?
- With what types of students, clients, participants, staff do you think the program is most/least effective?
- What is the program's theory of action?
- What are the policy alternatives if the program is found effective? How much expansion is possible? How might expansion sites be selected?
- What are the possible markets, communities, or sites for future expansion?
- What are the policy alternatives if the program is found ineffective? Would the program be cutback, eliminated, and/or refined?

You will notice that some of the questions are the same for both formative and summative efforts, those dealing with the key features of the program and its most significant outcomes. Summative evaluators, like formative evaluators, need to understand the distinguishing characteristics of program processes or implementation so they can document whether or not the program in fact occurred. But while the formative evaluator focuses on identifying those aspects of a program that might productively change, the summative evaluator focuses on clarifying the policy directions that are likely to result from different scenarios—for example, if the program is found to be uniformly successful, or if the program is successful only with particular types of participants. Posing a number of "what if" questions can help policymakers articulate the relevant issues.

Outline the Services You Can Provide

In accomplishing Phase A you will want to convey to the key decision makers and users a preliminary description of what you can and cannot do for them within the constraints of your time, budget, and the exigencies of the program and its context. Almost always you will find that a number of alternative configurations of evaluation activities are possible and in fact equally attractive, each carrying with it a number of advantages as well as disadvantages. The potential variety in role is particularly great if you are functioning as a formative evaluator working toward program improvement; do you want to act primarily as a researcher, a subject matter expert, a facilitator for problem solving, a synthesizer, a disseminator of information or public relations promoter, a group process leader or organizational facilitator? Consider your areas of greatest competence and those in which you lack expertise as well as, of course, the primary needs of the program. Your information users should know in what ways you believe you can be of most benefit to the program as well as how the program might profit from the services of a consultant who could handle matters outside your expertise.

In any event you may want to give your funders/users the opportunity to select from among several options. Even if you have a single evaluation plan in mind, consider offering a number of alternatives, presenting your preferences and their rationale as recommendations, and then negotiating the general form your evaluation will take. Try not to become enmeshed in details too early, particularly for your formative role. In this case, you need only agree initially on an outline of your evaluation responsibilities. As the program develops, these plans could easily change in response to programmatic changes, problems which emerge, and so on.

When describing the services you might perform, list the kinds of questions you will try to answer about such issues as goals, implementation of program activities or services, adequacy of administrative and management procedures, productivity, changes in performance or in attitudes. Describe, as well, the supporting data you will gather to back up depictions of program events and outcomes.

If you are conducting a summative evaluation, you also will need to propose particular evaluation designs for the data collection methods you plan to use. Be prepared to describe how the designs will increase the power and interpretability of the data. Be sure also to discuss the administrative requirements underlying your proposed design(s), and the potential tradeoffs between administrative feasibility and technical quality.

You also may want to propose quantitative designs in formative evaluation situations where you note controversy over the inclusion of a program component, or where there exists a set of programmatic alternatives without a persuasive reason to favor any one of them. In these cases, suggest pilot studies based on *planned variations*. These studies, which could last just a few weeks, would introduce competing variations in the program at different sites. To help planners or managers eventually choose among them, you would compare their ease of installation, their relative effect on outcomes and on staff and participant satisfaction. Planned variation studies for a program under development from scratch might emphasize the relative effectiveness of different approaches and activities. Where a previously designed program is being adapted to a new locale, planned variation studies will more likely look at variations in staffing patterns and program management.

Whether your focus is formative or summative, as the last chapter advised, you will want to suggest a balanced set of data collection activities, covering program context,

implementation, outcomes, and costs. Where possible, you will want to use a variety of data collection methods and of informant sources to examine each aspect. Where your interests are formative, consider continuous monitoring of program implementation and periodic checks on outcomes and satisfaction. Try to be sure also that your plan includes at least one service to the program that requires your frequent presence at program sites and staff meetings. This will help you stay abreast of and sensitive to what is happening and will enable you to maintain continuous rapport and communication with the staff. Such extensive contact with staff is generally not necessary for a summative evaluation.

Document your agreement. Once you and your clients have reached a preliminary agreement about your role and activities, write it down. This will avoid wasting time and effort in lengthy grandiose planning activities that miss the mark in terms of sponsor needs or budgets. Your tentative scope of work statement at this point should include the following:

- a description of the evaluation questions you will address;
- the data collection methods you have planned;
- your understanding of the tasks and responsibilities that program staff or others will undertake;
- required reports; and
- budget available for the study.

You will notice that your agreement requires that you generally think through the planning tasks you will accomplish in detail during Phase B. In some cases, such forecasting will be relatively easy; in other cases you may want to agree only on general approaches and on the total budget available for your study. In any event, the outcome of Phase B will be a design report and a more formal contract detailing your data collection plans. If your role is formative, be certain to stress the tentative nature of your outline, allowing for changes in the program and in the needs of the staff.

Phase B: Select Appropriate Evaluation Methods

In Phase A, you established a common understanding with your study sponsor(s) and, where appropriate, with program staff and other information users about the purposes of the evaluation and about the nature of its activities. In Phase B, those understandings are fleshed out into a clearly specified, program-sensitive set of data collection procedures and, where relevant, measurement instruments. The program description you produced in Phase A serves as a reference point for all your evaluation procedures.

If you are conducting a formative evaluation and are faced with a fuzzy program plan, you will start by helping planners and staff to better articulate their intentions. With a refined program description in hand, you then will need to complete a number of closely interrelated steps in order to plan your evaluation and data collection strategies, including targeting exactly what is to be observed or measured and when, choosing an appropriate design(s), selecting or developing suitable measurement instruments/evaluation methods, conceiving a sampling strategy, and making plans to ensure a timely data collection effort.

The specification of your evaluation procedures involves a complex interplay between a number of interlocking decisions about

- the specific aspects of program context, processes, and outcomes on which your study will focus;
- the best feasible methods to measure or otherwise observe those program aspects (specific measurement instruments you will purchase or develop and/or sources of information for other data collection methods);
- the design and sampling plan for administering or enacting your chosen methods; and
- the logistical plan that will enable you to complete your evaluation tasks within a specified schedule.

The set of steps you need to complete is generally the same regardless of whether your role is formative or summative; in either case you will want to focus attention on *collecting information of greatest interest and use to your primary user(s) about the most significant aspects of the program and its outcomes in a way that ensures the quality, validity, and reliability of the information you collect.* The flavor of your data collection plans, the timing and frequency of data collection efforts, and the concerns of greatest interest to you, however, will vary significantly depending on your role.

If You Are Concentrating on Summative Concerns

As a summative evaluator, your primary concerns are documenting or assessing program effects and determining their causes and generalizability. These concerns likely will cause you to emphasize program outcomes over program implementation and may well encourage you to emphasize experimental or quasi-experimental designs in your data collection efforts. As in the program description, your attention will be focused not on the details of implementation or on the objectives and subobjectives each program component is supposed to foster but rather on documenting major patterns or constellations of activities and on examining the program's success with end-of-program outcomes. Because you are concerned with documenting these major patterns and outcomes, you may not need to pay much attention to how or at what specific times they evolve and therefore will not need to collect data at close intervals throughout the program. (You may very well want, however, to collect longitudinal data, requiring data collection at more than one point in time.) For a summative evaluation, the challenge of planning your evaluation methods involves decisions about what to measure or observe and how best to measure or observe it; you then figure out

how to implement your decisions using the best possible design plan. Unfortunately, there are no simple rules for making such decisions about what and how. The following rules of thumb, however, are offered as a rough guide:

(1) Focus data collection where you are most likely to uncover program effects if any occur.
(2) Try to collect a variety of information.
(3) Try to think of imaginative—and credible—ways to detect achievement of program objectives.
(4) Collect information to show that the program at least has done no harm.
(5) Measure or observe what you think your sponsor and other users will look for when they receive your report.
(6) Try to measure or observe things that will advance the development of sound theories of practice.

Use of each of these pointers is discussed below.

Focus data collection where you are most likely to uncover program effects, if any occur. While it is important that the evaluation tries in some way to acknowledge and to assess major but perhaps ambitious or distant goals, you may not want to emphasize them when deciding what to observe or measure. One way to decide how to focus the evaluation is to classify program goals according to the time frame in which they can be expected to be achieved and the feasibility of their attainment given the number of influences that are beyond the program control. Any particular intervention or program is more likely to demonstrate a detectable effect on proximate outcomes rather than those either logically or temporally remote. In addition, you reduce the possibility that the program will show effects if you focus on outcomes whose attainment is likely to be hampered by uncontrolled features of the situation. You should look for the program's effects close to the time of the program treatment, and you should measure objectives that the program as implemented seeks to achieve.

Consider, for example, a hypothetical situation in which a social service training program has been designed with the objective of increasing the diagnostic and communication skills of staff working in programs for at-risk, inner-city juveniles. The program was instituted in order to eventually accomplish these primary goals:

- to increase the number of appropriate referrals to other helping agencies;
- to encourage positive attitudes about the agency among clients and the community; and
- to reduce the juvenile delinquency rate.

In evaluating this program, you could assess the number of appropriate referrals and the juvenile delinquency rate in the community before, during, and after the program. You also could collect client attitude data before and after. These, after all, reflect the program's impact on its major goals.

There is a problem with basing the evaluation solely on these goals, however. Judgments of the quality of the program will then be based only on the program's apparent effect on these outcomes. While these are the major outcomes of interest, they are remote effects likely to come about through a long chain of events which the employee training program has only begun. A better evaluation would also include attention to whether employees learned what was intended from the training program itself or whether they displayed the behaviors the training was designed to produce.

In general, since there are various ways in which a program can affect its participants, one of the evaluator's most valuable contributions might be to determine at what level the program has had an effect. Think of a program as potentially affecting people in three different ways:

(1) *At minimum, it can make members of the target group aware that its services are available.* Prospective participants can simply learn that the program is taking place and that an effort is being made to address their needs. In some situations, demonstrating that the target audience has been informed that the program is accessible to them might be important. This will be the case particularly with programs that rely on voluntary enrollment, such as lifelong learning programs, a venereal disease education program, or community outreach programs for seniors or juveniles. Evaluation of these kinds of programs will require a check on the quality of their publicity.

(2) *A program can impart useful information.* A program's most valuable outcome might be that it conveys information to some group. Learning, of course, is the major objective of most educational programs. Although most programs aim toward loftier goals than just the receipt of information, attention should not be diverted from assessing whether the less ambitious effects occurred. In the employee training example, for instance, it would be important to show that employees have become more aware of the problems and life experiences of minority clients. If you are unable to show an impact on their behavior, you can at least show that the program has taught them something.

(3) *A program can actually influence changes in behavior.* The most difficult evaluation to undertake is one that looks for the influence of a program on people's day-to-day behavior. While behavior and attitude change are at the top of the list of many program objectives, determining whether such changes have occurred often requires more of an effort that the evaluator can muster. You will, of course, be interested in at least keeping tabs on whether the program is achieving some of its grander goals. Consider yourself warned, however, that the probability of a program showing a powerful behavioral effect often is minimal.

Try to collect a variety of information. Three good strategies will help you do this. First, try to find useful information which is going to be collected anyhow. Find out which assessments are given as part of the program or routinely in the setting; look at records from the program or at reports, journals, and logs which are to be kept. Check to see whether evidence of the achievement of some of the program's objectives can be inferred from these.

Another good way to increase the amount of information you can collect is by finding someone to collect information for you. You might persuade program staff to establish record-keeping systems that will benefit both your evaluation and their program. You might hire someone such as a student from a local high school or college to collect information. Perhaps you can even persuade a graduate student seeking a topic for a research study to choose one whose data collection will coincide with your evaluation.

Finally, a good way to increase the kinds of information you are able to collect is to use sampling procedures. They will cut down the costs and time you must spend administering and processing any single measure. Choosing representative sites, events, or participants on which to focus, or randomly sampling groups for testing or surveys, will usually produce information as credible to your audiences as if you had looked at the entire population of people served.

Collecting a variety of information gives you the advantage of presenting a thorough look at the program. It also gives you a good chance of finding indicators of significant program effects and of collecting evidence to corroborate some of your shakier findings.

Besides accumulating a breadth of information about the program, you might decide to conduct case studies to give your picture of the program greater depth and sensitivity. The case study evaluator, interested in the broad range of events and relationships which affect participants in the program, chooses to examine closely particular cases—that is, a school, an office, a particular group, or even an individual. This method enables the evaluator to examine the proportionate influence of the program among the myriad other factors influencing the actions and feelings of the people under study. Case studies will give your audience a strong notion of the flavor of the activities and services which constituted the program and of the way in which these activities fit into the daily experiences of participants.

Try to think of imaginative—and credible—ways to detect achievement of program objectives. Suppose in the staff training example discussed earlier it turns out that referral rates have increased only slightly and attitudes as measured have remained unchanged. These findings make the program look ineffective.

It might be the case, however, that though staff have continued their referrals at the same rate, they are providing the receiving agencies with more detailed and suggestive diagnostic information, have established better working relationships with a variety of agencies, and are spending more time talking with their clients and community members. Furthermore, while referral rates are unchanged, more clients are following up on their referrals.

A little thought to the more mundane ways in which the program might affect participants could lead you to collect key information about program effects. A good way to uncover nonobvious but important indicators of program impact is to ask participants during the course of the evaluation about changes they have seen occurring. Where an informal report uncovers an intriguing effect, check the generality of this person's perception by means of a quick questionnaire, a test of a sample of participants, and analyses of your own observations. You should, incidentally, try to keep a little money in the evaluation budget to finance such ad hoc data-gathering.

Collect information to show that the program at least has done no harm. In deciding what to measure, keep in mind the possible objections of skeptics or of the program's critics. A common objection is that the time spent taking part in the program might have been better spent pursuing another activity. Sometimes the evaluation of a program, therefore, will need to attend to the issue of whether participants, by spending time in the program, may have missed some other important opportunity or experience. This is often the case with programs which remove participants from their usual environment to take part in special activities. "Pull-out" programs of this kind in schools are often directed toward students with special needs—either enrichment or remediation. You may need to show, for instance, that students who take part in a speech therapy program during reading time have not suffered in their reading achievement. Similarly, you may need to show that an accelerated junior high school science program has not actually prevented students from learning science concepts usually taught at this level.

Related to the problem of demonstrating that participants have not missed opportunities is the requirement that you also show the program did no actual harm. For instance, attitude programs aimed at human relations skills or people's self-perceptions could conceivably go awry and provoke neuroses. Where your audience is likely to express concern about these matters, you should anticipate the concern by looking for these effects yourself.

Gear your data collection to what you think your sponsor or other users will look for when they receive your report. Try to get to know the stakeholders who are expected to use your evaluation information. Find out what they most want to know. Are they, for instance, more concerned about the proper implementation of the program than about its outcomes? A parent advisory group, for instance, might wish to see an open classroom functioning in the school. They may be more concerned with the installation of the program than with student

achievement, at least during the first year of operation. In this case, your evaluation should pay more attention to assessing program implementation than to outcomes. If you get to know your primary audience, you will realize that, for instance, Mr. Johnson on the Board of Trustees always wants to know about integration or interpersonal understanding, or that the foundation funding your study is mainly concerned with potential job skills. Visualize members of your primary audiences reading or hearing your report; try to put yourself in their place. Think of the questions you would ask the evaluator if you were them.

Focus data collection on things you can feasibly measure or observe. Rare if ever will be the case, as discussed in the last chapter, that evaluators will have unlimited time or resources to complete their tasks; often their access to sites, to particular data sources, or to staff and client time and cooperation will likewise be limited. These constraints coupled with the limits of assessment technologies themselves (e.g., the validity and reliability of available assessment instruments) lead to the obvious dictum: plan to measure or observe only those things which you can feasibly measure or observe with some degree of reliability and validity. The rule is equally applicable, of course, regardless of whether your role is formative or summative.

Try to measure or observe things that will advance the development of sound theories of practice. The search for generalizable findings about program effectiveness— does this program work and is it likely to work in other similar settings?—is a driving force behind many summative evaluations and one which encourages the use of experimental, or at least quasi-experimental, designs. Generalizable statements about program effectiveness, where they can be made, in and of themselves can contribute to theory development by providing positive examples for analysis and replication. More specific contributions to theory can be made, however, by explicitly examining those things which major models or theories of the field hold as most important in effective practice.

Many programs are systematically designed, in fact, to implement the tenets of a model or theory of behavior. Examples abound in all types of programs:

- behavioral and reinforcement theories which may underlie instructional, discipline, substance abuse, diet, and a range of other programs;
- theories of anomie which may underlie dropout or suicide prevention programs;
- models of organization (e.g., quality circles) that prescribe arrangements and procedures for effective practice;
- group process models which underlie social action and other intervention programs;
- counseling models which may underlie programs for deviant behavior.

Each of these models or theories explicates the particular factors and processes which its proponents believe are essential to promote certain desirable outcomes. By focusing your data collection on these critical variables, your evaluation can provide an actual *test* of the theory's validity, and/or can identify those variables which seem to make the most difference in program success. (This is particularly the case if your evaluation is based on a strong research design.)

Basing your evaluation on credible theories of practice has dual benefits: it focuses attention on things that are likely to make a difference in program operations and outcomes, and it encourages studies which can have impact and contribute to effective practice beyond the particular program(s) under inquiry.

If You Are Concentrating on Formative Concerns

Many of these same rules of thumb also will be applicable in a formative evaluation—for example, be creative about how to assess program process and outcomes, try to gather a variety of types and sources of information, focus data collection on those areas where the program is most likely to make a difference, measure or observe those things your principal users (program designers and staff) are most interested in. Your primary decision rule for planning your formative evaluation strategy, however, will be to select those strategies which best enable you to:

- pinpoint areas of program strength and weakness;
- refine and revise program plans and, if necessary, your evaluation plan;
- hypothesize about cause-effect relationships between program features and outcomes; and
- draw conclusions about the relative effectiveness of program components or of alternative approaches.

The degree to which your own personal opinions should guide your data collection and reporting, incidentally, is something to be negotiated with staff and planners. You could, on the one hand, take the stance of an impartial conduit for the information the staff feels it needs. At the other extreme, you could develop strong opinions, calling staff attention to what you feel are the program's most critical and problematic processes and outcomes. In the former situation, your report will convey the data you collected to program planners with the postscript "Now *you* make the decision." If you plan to express opinions, then your reports will likely advocate a course of action and the data collected will be planned to provide evidence in support of your case.

In either instance, the ideal evaluation procedure for a formative evaluator probably would be to remain on site with the program for extended periods of time, in the style of the participant-observer, in order to observe program processes and to take repeated assessments of progress en route to end-of-program outcomes. Realistically, how-

ever, it is likely that budget, time, and possibly the geographical distribution of program sites will make such vigilance impossible. You will have to rely on sampling, good rapport with the staff and others, and on a well-designed measurement/observation plan to give you an ongoing and accurate picture of the program and its effects.

Your major source of firsthand information about the program will be your own informal observations and conversations with staff members while on site. Their descriptions of the program and explanations of what you see occurring should give you a good idea of how to design more formal data-gathering instruments. Informal observations should also show where the program is going well and where it is failing, where a program component has been efficiently carried out, where it is partially implemented, and where it is not taking place.

In order to ensure that your informal impressions are representative and accurate, more formal data-gathering will be necessary. For the purpose of formative evaluation, three approaches to collecting data about the program have been found useful:

- periodic program monitoring
- component analysis
- pilot and feasibility studies

Your choice will be primarily determined by what you want to know.

Periodic program monitoring. The formative evaluator who wishes to check whether a program is implemented according to plan or how it evolves throughout the evaluation selects a target set of characteristics or general processes which are then monitored periodically and at various sites. Outcome measures also may be administered at these times to see whether there is progress toward the attainment of objectives of interest to the staff. The sites supplying formative information and the times at which this information is collected are often based on a sampling plan to ensure that the data collection intervals reflect the program as a whole.

Example. Leonard Pierson, assistant to a district's Director of Research and Evaluation, was asked to serve as formative evaluator during the first year of a parent education program. The purpose of the program was to train parents of preschool children to tutor them at home in skills related to reading readiness: classification of objects, concept formation, basic math and counting, conversation and vocabulary. Federal funds had been provided for the training and to purchase home workbooks which were supplied free of charge. These workbooks sequenced and structured the home tutoring. They contained lessons, suggestions for enrichment activities, and short periodic assessment tests. The parent training centers were set up at six community agencies and schools throughout the district. Local teachers conducted evening classes to teach parents to use the workbooks daily with their children at home.

When the project director contacted Mr. Pierson, he was simply asked to give whatever formative evaluation help he could. Mr. Pierson, free to define his own role, decided to focus on four questions:

- Most important, do students learn the skills that are emphasized by the workbook?
- To what extent do parents actually work with their child daily?
- Do parents use techniques taught to them in the training course, or do they develop their own?
- Are their own techniques more or less effective than those they have been trained to use?

In order to help answer these questions, Mr. Pierson designed two instruments and a monitoring system for administering them periodically:

- a general achievement test consisting of items sampled from the progress tests in the workbooks. The test will be administered every six weeks to a sample of participants' children. Presumably scores on this test should increase over time. A control group will also take the test every six weeks to account for learning due to sheer maturation.
- an observation instrument to be completed by the community member who visits the home to give the six weekly achievement tests. The instrument records the amount of progress made in the workbooks since the last visit, the nature of the teaching methods used by the apparent appropriateness of the parent, and current lesson to the student's skills—that is, whether it seems to be too difficult. Observers will be trained to be particularly alert to changes in teaching style, recording both deviations and innovations.

The details of a periodic monitoring plan are usually agreed to by the evaluator and planners at the beginning of the formative evaluation and then vary little throughout the evaluator's collaboration with the program. The periodic program monitor submits interim reports at the conclusion of each data-gathering phase. Like Table 3, these often start with whether the program is on schedule but also include whether impediments to the program have been detected, whether the staff and others are experiencing difficulties, and so on, and for each the reports consider possible reasons why.

A formative evaluator might use something like Table 3 to report to the program director and the staff at each location the results of monthly site visits. Each interim report could include an updated table accompanied by explanations of why ratings of N (needs attention) have been assigned. The occasion at which assessments are made are determined by the passage of standard intervals—a month, a semester—or by logical transition periods in the program, such as the dates of completion of critical units. The evaluator might check time and again at the same sites or with the same people, or could select a different representative sample to provide data at each occasion.

TABLE 3

Project Monitoring: Activities

Objective: To institute a clearinghouse facility for runaway youths.

Objective 6: By February 28, 19YY, operational plans will be completed for establishing the clearinghouse.

Winona City Division of Child Services

Planned Activities	19XX				19YY			
	Sep	Oct	Nov	Dec	Jan	Feb	Mar	Apr
6.1 Identify staff to participate		I	C					
6.2 Selected staff members review ideas, goals, and other projects		I	P	P	C			
6.3 Identify client needs		N	I	P	C			
6.4 Identify community services		N	I	P	C			
6.5 Identify staff needs and skills		N	I	P	C			
6.6 Evaluate data collected in 6.3-6.5						I	N	C
6.7 Identify and prioritize goals and objectives for the clearinghouse			I	N	P	P	C	
6.8 Identify policies and operating procedures		N	I	P	P	C		

Evaluator's periodic progress rating:
I = activity initiated   P = satisfactory progress
C = activity completed   N = needs attention

SOURCE: This table has been adapted from a formative monitoring procedure by Marvin C. Alkin.

Where the same measures or observations are used repeatedly at the same sites, periodic monitoring resembles a time series research design. This permits the evaluator to form a defensible interpretation of the program's role in bringing about the changes in outcomes. Using a control group whose progress is also monitored further helps the evaluator to estimate how program participants would be performing if there were no program—although this approach probably is the exception rather than the rule. More often, a more qualitative approach will be used.

Component analysis. An evaluator can focus on individual units or segments of the program that the staff has identified as particularly critical or problematic. In this case, monitoring of implementation will require in-depth scrutiny of the particular program component under study and an analysis of its strengths and weaknesses. Because the evaluator's task is to determine the success and value of specific program components, the implementation and effects of these components will need to be described in as detailed a way as possible. Achievement measures, attitude instruments, and other outcome indicators, coupled with observations and interviews, will have to be sensitive to the specific objectives that the components of interest address. This could make it necessary for the evaluator to tailor-make a test, since general attitude, achievement, or other performance measures will be unlikely to address the particular outcomes of interest. In some cases, in-program testing may be a built-in feature of the program—for example, drug treatment programs which require periodic testing, end-of-unit tests found in many curriculum materials, or physical health indicators routinely gathered in many fitness programs. The occasions on which assessments are made are determined by when important components occur during the course of the program and their duration. Sampling of representative *sites* and *participants* should be done where it is inadvisable or impractical to assess everyone. Analyzing the process and effectiveness of the components for particular subgroups may be revealing.

Pilot and feasibility studies. These are usually undertaken because members of the program staff or its planners have in mind a particular set of issues that they need to settle or have a hard decision to make. Pilot and feasibility studies are carefully conducted and are usually experimental; they judge the relative quality of two or more ways to implement a particular program component. Pilot studies could be undertaken, for instance, to determine the most effective order in which to present information in a science discovery lab or the most beneficial time to switch patients from inpatient to outpatient status. These studies require that different, competing versions of a program component be installed at various sites. The evaluator first checks the degree to which each site carried out the program variation it was assigned; then, after giving the variation time to produce the results, the evaluator tests for their relative effectiveness. Like unit testing, feasibility studies demand assessment instruments that are sensitive to the specific outcomes that the program versions aim to produce. Random sampling is highly desirable since feasibility studies often use statistical tests to look for significant differences in the performance of groups experiencing different program variations. Pilot tests generally take place either before the program has begun, or ad hoc throughout the course of the evaluation whenever controversy or lack of information creates a need to try variations of the program.

Example 1. Dr. Schwartz, a university professor working as a formative evaluator for educational television station KDKC, overheard a conversation one day between two writers working on an episode for a series on cultural awareness. "Poverty and Potatoes is a silly name for an episode in Ireland," one writer was saying. "Well, maybe you can do better; but I say we need catchy titles—things that will make the kids want to watch," the other writer retorted. Dr. Schwartz offered to help the writers find such a title. He suggested that for each episode of the program, they write four or five possible titles. He would then construct and administer a questionnaire for students in order to find out from the target audience which title would most entice them to watch a television program.

Example 2. The Stone City Council voted in January to fund a new program to deal with the city's increasing problems with runaway youths. The Children Protection Agency was charged with responsibility for planning and instituting the new program. After considerable analysis, they concluded that many of the runaways inhabiting the city streets were falling through the cracks and were not being served by the various agencies and service organizations available to help them. The youths themselves did not know of these available services, and police and other interested groups were not sufficiently informed about the services most appropriate for different youths. They agreed on the vital need for a central location where all runaways could be referred for service. There was strong disagreement, however, about whether this centralized locale should function only as a referral agency or should also provide in-house counseling services. Some members of the group argued vehemently that these youths had already been shuffled around enough; others were equally adamant that quality services available in other locales should not be unnecessarily duplicated. The program's evaluator, Ms. Cortino, intervened and suggested they test the viability of the two ideas.

The two alternative approaches were piloted. Collaborative arrangements with external agencies brought counselors to the clearinghouse on alternative days. Youths referred to the clearinghouse during these times received counseling on site and were encouraged to continue to attend counseling on site during the specified hours. Youths coming to the clearinghouse on alternative days were referred to other counselors close by in the neighborhood. After three months, the two approaches were compared on client and staff satisfaction, on persistence in counseling, and on life changes.

Pilot and feasibility tests usually occur only when the evaluator suggests them. Planners do not usually ask to have this sort of service performed for them. A feasibility study need not be based on outcomes. A common question it might address is "Will people like Version X better than Version Y?"

Whatever plan you use for monitoring the program's process and effects, your efforts will allow the staff to make data-based judgments about whether program procedures are having the desired effect on participants, staff, and others. Besides the outcomes that planners hope to produce, you will need to look vigilantly for unintended outcomes, side-effects that can be ascribed to the program but which have not been mentioned by planners or listed in official documents. Although side-effects are generally thought of as detrimental, they could as easily be beneficial. You might discover, for example, potentially effective practices spontaneously implemented at a few sites that are worth exporting to others. Negative unintended effects are important to discover if the program is to be improved. They highlight areas that require added attention, modification, or even discarding.

Remember that when the data you collect suggest revisions in the program, you will have to amend the program description as well. Program staff should take part in making these revisions, and consensus should be reached before any changes are recorded in the program's official description. New program statements may also suggest revisions or additions to your contracted evaluation activities.

Arrive at a Final Contract

Phase B produces a complete set of plans and schedules for conducting your evaluation. Armed with these specific plans, you are in a position to estimate with some precision the anticipated costs of the evaluation and to commit firmly to specific procedures and reports. The final step of Phase B then is to make your agreements and commitment formal, filling in the details of your Phase A preliminary agreement. Your agreement should include the following:

- a description of the evaluation questions you will address;
- the data collection you have planned, including sources, site, instruments or other data collection methods;
- a timeline for these activities, such as the one in Table 4;
- list of the tasks and responsibilities you expect program staff or others to undertake in support of your evaluation;
- schedule of reports and meetings, including tentative agendas where possible;
- a budget estimating anticipated costs.

Remember you will be responsible for the timely completion of all evaluation activities contracted. Exercise your options to accept or reject assignments and scale your evaluation accordingly.

Phase C: Collect and Analyze Information

During this phase, the data collection and analysis plans proposed in Phase B are put into effect. By this time, what remains is to see that everything proceeds as planned: that deadlines are met; that design and sampling plans are implemented properly; that instruments are administered, interviews and observations conducted and coded; that data are analyzed. Depending on whether your procedures are generally quantitative or principally qualitative, or a combination of the two, the stream of process during this phase will vary considerably. Where your approach is more qualitative, you will move back and forth between collecting your data and analyzing them, engaging in an interactive inductive process as you refine the answers to your evaluation questions. The process of those evaluators playing a more formative role also will be more fluid, engaging in repeated cycles of data collection, analysis, and reporting. Whether your approach is more quantitative or more qualitative, more fluid or more linear, you will want to ensure that your analysis techniques are valid and well justified and that your interpretations are well grounded in available data. *How to Use Qualitative Methods in Evaluation* and *How to Analyze Data* provide more detail on these methods.

Phase D: Report Findings

The reporting mode for evaluations varies with the situation. As is shown in Table 5, formative reports almost never look like the more technical ones submitted by summative evaluators. A summative report is most often a written, formal summary of a program's implementation and effects. It may or may not be accompanied by an oral report. While most are familiar with this type of formal report, reporting in formative situations bears some clarification.

Much of formative reporting takes place in conversations or discussions that the evaluator has with individuals or groups of program personnel. The form of your report will depend on:

- the reporting style that is most comfortable to you and the staff with whom you are working;
- the extent to which official records are required;
- whether you will disseminate results only among program sites, or to interested outsiders and the general community as well;
- how soon the information must reach its users in order to be useful; and
- how the information will be used.

Whether reports are oral or written is up to you and the needs of your situation. Remember, however, that if additional planning or program modification will be based on the reports you give, then it is best to *discuss* your findings with the staff, perhaps at a problem-solving meeting, so that remedies for problems can be debated and decisions made. The *Program Evaluation Kit* book *How to Communicate Evaluation Findings* should be of great help as you plan reporting strategies, balancing the requirements and benefits of written reports and other less formal mechanisms.

A written report is a document of activities and findings to which your users can continually refer and which can be used in program planning and revision. Lengthy written reports, however, take time to draft, polish, discuss, and revise; this may be time that could be better spent collecting information and helping staff with program development. In many cases, you may find that the best way to leave a written trace of your formative work will be to document your findings in memos and to periodically revise the program description you produced.

In contrast to written reports, face-to-face meetings provide the staff and planners with a forum for active involvement in program planning and evaluation, for discussion, clarification, and detailed elaboration of the evaluation's findings as well as the opportunity for making suggestions about upcoming evaluation activities. During such conversational reports, you also will be able to ask for help, if needed, in solving logistical problems or in collecting data. Staff members should also be encour-

TABLE 4

Sample Timeline of the Formative Evaluator's Responsibilities

Tasks/Activities	Time in Months 19XX (J J A S O N D) / 19YY (J F M A M)	Completion Date	Reports and Deliverables	Program Evaluator	Program Director	Teaching Staff	Principals	Teacher Aides	Clerical Staff
Review/revision of program plan	(bar)	July 31	Revised written plan	37	8	—	6	—	16
Discussion about method of formative feedback alternatives	(bar)	Sept 15	None	16	7	24	6	—	—
Planning of implementation-monitoring activities	(bar)	Sept 30	List of instruments; Schedule of classroom visits	60	10	24	—	—	2
Construction of implementation instruments	(bar)	Oct 10	Completed instruments	60	5	12	—	—	16
Planning of unit tests	(bar)	Oct 10	List and schedule of achievement tests	30	5	—	—	—	2
First meeting with staff	(bar)	Nov 1	None	9	15	24	2	20	—
First meeting with district administration	(bar)	Nov 8	First interim report	22	20	—	—	—	30
			TOTAL PERSON HOURS						

Number of personnel work hours consumed

TABLE 5

Contrasts Between Reports for Formative and Summative Evaluation

	Formative Report	Summative Report
Purpose	Shows the results of monitoring the program's implementation or of pilot tests conducted during the course of the program's installation. Intended to help change something going on in the program that is not working as well as it might, or to expand a practice or special activity that shows promise.	Documents the program's implementation either at the conclusion of a developmental period or after it has had sufficient time to undergo refinement and work smoothly. Intended to put the program on record, to describe it as a finished work.
Tone	Informal	Usually formal
Form	Can be written or audivisual; can be delivered to a group as a speech, or take the form of informal conversations with the project director or staff, etc.	Nearly always written, although some formal, verbal presentation might be made to supplement or explain the report's conclusions
Length	Variable	Variable, but sufficiently condensed or summarized so that it can be used to help planners or decision makers who have little time to spend reading at a highly detailed level.
Level of specificity	High, focusing on particular activities or materials used by particular people, or on what happened with with particular participants and at a certain place or point in time.	Usually more moderate, attempting to document general program characteristics common to many sites so that many summary statements and general overall decisions can be made.

aged to express problems they perceive or to suggest new information needs.

A schedule for interim reports, whether oral or written, should be part of the formative evaluation contract. Scheduled to accommodate program staffs' desire for information, such reports can include feedback of different sorts. At minimum, reports will simply describe what the formative evaluator saw taking place—what the program looked like and what achievement or attitudes appeared to result from it. Depending on this person's presumed expertise in such matters, the formative evaluator may also make suggestions about changes, point to places where the program is in particular need, and offer services to help remedy these problems. Your contributions along these lines will depend on your expertise and the contract you have worked out with the planners and staff.

If your evaluation service has focused on pilot or feasibility studies, then your report will follow a more standard outline, although you may supplement the discussion of the results with recommendations for adaptation, adoption, or rejection of certain program components and perhaps outline further studies that are needed.

The need to continually analyze and improve program components and arrangements should be a recurring theme in your conversations with and reports to the staff. You will find that once the staff are comfortable with program procedures, they may become complacent and may want to avoid making further changes in the program. The formative evaluator will have to make a conscious effort to keep the staff interested in looking at program activities and procedures with a view toward making them yet more appropriate, effective, and appealing for the participants. Although evaluators will have the responsibility of overseeing the collection of information to support decisions about program revisions, the suggestions and active involvement of planners and staff in this decision-making process are crucial. Everyone on the program staff should understand why the formative evaluation is occurring and should be encouraged to take part.

Involving the evaluation user in the reporting process is important for summative evaluations as well. It is always a good idea to let sponsors and other primary users read your report in draft form so they can indicate areas in need of greater clarification or analysis or point out places where misunderstandings have occurred. Depending on the situation, you may also want to give program representatives the opportunity to give such feedback. In any event, plan time in your schedule for a review draft, a period for review and comment, and subsequent revision time prior to submission of your final report.

For Further Reading

Alkin, M. C. (1985). *A guide for evaluation decision makers.* Newbury Park, CA: Sage.

Baker, E. L., & Saloutos, A. G. (1974). *Evaluating instructional programs.* Los Angeles: Center for the Study of Evaluation.

Brinkerhoff, R. O., Brethower, D. M., Hluchyj, T., & Nowakowski, J. R. (1983). *Program evaluation: Sourcebook, casebook—a practitioner's guide for trainers and educators.* Boston: Kluwer-Nijhoff.

Cooley, W., & Bickel, W. (1985). *Decision-oriented educational research.* Boston: Kluwer-Nijhoff.

Dawson, J. A., & D'Amico, J. J. (1985). Involving program staff in evaluation studies: A strategy for increasing use and enriching the data base. *Evaluation Review,* 9(2): 173-188.

Dickey, B., & Hampton, E. (1981). Effective problem-solving for evaluation utilization. *Knowledge: Creation, Diffusion, Utilization,* 2(3): 361-374.

Kantor, R. (1983). *The change masters.* New York: Simon & Schuster.

Lichfield, N., Kettle, P., & Whitbread, M. (1975). *Evaluation in the planning process.* Oxford: Pergamon Press.

Patton, M. Q. (1986). *Utilization-focused evaluation* (2nd ed.). Newbury Park, CA: Sage.

Pressman, J. L., & Wildavsky, A. (1984). *Implementation.* Berkeley: University of California Press.

Rossi, P., & Freeman, H. (1985). *Evaluation* (3rd ed.). Newbury Park, CA: Sage.

Williams, W., & Elmore, R. F. (1976). *Social program implementation.* New York: Academic Press.

Chapter 3
Step-by-Step Guides for Conducting a Formative Evaluation

Chapter 2 listed some of the myriad jobs of the formative evaluator. This role, it was mentioned, is most easily described in terms of the goal the formative evaluator has in mind—to collect and share with program managers, planners, and staff information that will lead to the modification or improvement of a program. The diversified nature of formative evaluation might make providing a step-by-step guide seem a little silly or arbitrary. In truth, there is no step-by-step way to perform the tasks involved with the role.

Enough activities are common among formative evaluators, however, to permit a general outline of what needs to be accomplished. Chapter 2 described four phases to which any formative evaluator must attend to some degree:

- *Phase A: Set the Boundaries of the Evaluation;* that is, negotiate the scope of the data-gathering activities in which you will engage, the aspects of the program on which you will concentrate, and the responsibilities of your audience to cooperate in the collection of data and to use the information you supply.
- *Phase B: Select Appropriate Evaluation Methods;* including clarification of program goals and of the *rationale* describing why program activities are thought to lead to these goals, followed by plans for monitoring and analyzing the program.
- *Phase C: Collect and Analyze Information.* This includes periodic observations and assessments to examine program implementation and progress toward outcomes.
- *Phase D: Report Findings* about changes to be made in the program and about additional formative activities.

Included in this chapter are step-by-step guides for *each* of these phases. Each guide lists the major events that might take place in completing the phase. You can look at the step-by-step guides as a reminder of critical decisions that

need to be made while working at a particular stage of a formative evaluation. The step-by-step guides should prompt you to be thoughtful in planning what you do, collecting information, and talking with the program staff. Each guide can serve as a *checklist* to help you keep track of what you have completed in the process of serving the program and to give you ideas about where to go and what to do next.

As Chapter 2 mentioned, many of the tasks falling within the scope of the different phases actually may occur simultaneously or in an order other than that described by the step-by-step guide. In general, however, there will be some logical order to how your evaluation unfolds. You will do most of Phase A, for instance, before you begin Phase C; and the tasks of Phase D, since they involve reporting and sharing information, will likely occur toward the end of information-gathering cycles. Consider the step-by-step guides, then, a loose map of the activities formative evaluators might find themselves performing. You will almost certainly have to attend in some way to many of the tasks listed in each phase. Use the step-by-step guides as you like.

An important thing to notice about the phases is that they demand considerable sharing of information between the formative evaluator and his or her audience. Each phase produces a product. The product of the first phase, during which roles are defined and the evaluation gets started, is a preliminary agreement, or at least an outline, of the mutual responsibilities of the evaluator and the planners and staff. The product of the second phase is final agreement on evaluation plans (complete with goals, a description of program implementation, and a rationale), and ways each will be examined. Phase C, which includes *program monitoring,* probably the evaluator's major responsibility, produces analyzed and summarized information about program implementation and progress toward goals. Reporting of this information is so important to formative evaluation that it is relegated its own phase—Phase D.

If you are working as a formative evaluator for the first time in the setting, your best guidance might come from a conversation with someone who has evaluated the program before or who has served as a formative evaluator in a similar setting. If formative evaluation presents a change in the evaluation role to which you are accustomed, then seek out someone who has done it before. Nothing beats advice from long experience.

Whenever possible, the step-by-step guides use checklists and worksheets to help you keep track of what you have decided and found out. Actually, the worksheets might be better called "guidesheets" since you will have to copy many of them onto your own paper rather than use the one in the book. Space simply does not permit the book to provide places to list large quantities of data.

While the first edition of this *Evaluator's Handbook* focused specifically on evaluating educational programs, this second edition has been designed to meet the needs of a variety of fields. The quest for a more generic approach brings with it some loss in specific guidance and some problems in terminology, particularly in how to designate the various role groups commonly associated with particular programs: those on whom the program is targeted, those who deliver the program, those at various levels who may be responsible for program administration and/or decision making, and other significant constituencies. While no one set of terms perfectly fits all situations, we have chosen to use the following terminology:

Participants—those on whom the project's primary objectives are targeted, e.g., students, clients, patients, employees, residents, at-risk juveniles.

Staff—those primarily responsible for delivering the program to participants, e.g., teachers, clinicians, social workers, probation officers, trainers.

Site managers/administrators—those on-site supervisors responsible for managing overall operations, e.g., principals, supervisors, office managers, chief administrators.

Local or regional managers—those responsible for the operation of a number of local units or sites, e.g., district superintendents, county supervisors, regional directors, and/or administrative staff in intermediate unit settings.

Governing board—those holding fiduciary responsibility for the organization and its operations and/or charged with responsibility for policymaking, e.g., boards of education, boards of trustees.

Community members—significant others in the program environments who are related to the program and its participants, who may both affect and be affected by the program, e.g., parents, local businesses, public at large, other service providers.

Consider now how these terms relate to those in your program situation so that when you see them in the pages which follow, you can substitute the more specific, relevant nomenclature of your field.

As you use the guides, you will come upon references marked by the symbol ◣▷. These direct you to read sections of various *How to* books contained in the *Program Evaluation Kit*. At these junctures in the evaluation, it will be necessary for you to review a concept or follow a procedure outlined in one of these eight resource books:

- *How to Focus an Evaluation*
- *How to Design a Program Evaluation*
- *How to Use Qualitative Methods in Evaluation*
- *How to Assess Program Implementation*
- *How to Measure Attitudes*
- *How to Measure Performance and Use Tests*
- *How to Analyze Data*
- *How to Communicate Evaluation Findings*

To give you an overview of the formative evaluation tasks included in the guides, a flowchart showing the steps required to complete each phase appears at the beginning of each step-by-step guide.

Instructions

Phase A encompasses the evaluation planning period—from the time you accept the job of formative evaluator until you begin to actually carry out the assignments dictated by the role. Much of Phase A amounts to gaining an understanding of the program and outlining the services you can perform, then negotiating them with the members of the staff who will use your formative information.

Phase A is composed of six steps:

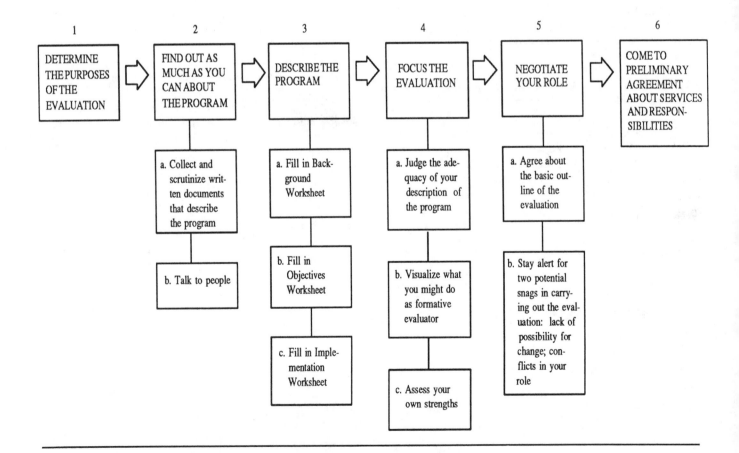

1	2	3	4	5	6
DETERMINE THE PURPOSES OF THE EVALUATION	FIND OUT AS MUCH AS YOU CAN ABOUT THE PROGRAM	DESCRIBE THE PROGRAM	FOCUS THE EVALUATION	NEGOTIATE YOUR ROLE	COME TO PRELIMINARY AGREEMENT ABOUT SERVICES AND RESPON-SIBILITIES
	a. Collect and scrutinize written documents that describe the program	a. Fill in Back-ground Worksheet	a. Judge the ade-quacy of your description of the program	a. Agree about the basic out-line of the evaluation	
	b. Talk to people	b. Fill in Objectives Worksheet	b. Visualize what you might do as formative evaluator	b. Stay alert for two potential snags in carry-ing out the eval-uation: lack of possibility for change; con-flicts in your role	
		c. Fill in Imple-mentation Worksheet	c. Assess your own strengths		

Determine the purposes of the evaluation

Instructions

The job of the formative evaluator is to collect, digest and share information with program managers, planners, and/or staff that will help them to improve their program. Usually, such information will enable the identification of:

- The strengths and weaknesses of the program or of any of its components

- Barriers to program implementation

- Impediments to program effectiveness

- Negative side-effects

As a result of such information, the primary audiences for the evaluation (managers, planners, staff) may decide to augment, modify, and/or delete certain components of the program; restructure or reorganize the program design; reorient program goals and objectives; and/or any number of actions that could be construed as improvement-oriented.

If your findings are supposed to answer particular questions or to address particular problematic issues, then you need to find out what these are. Then you will have to ensure that you collect the relevant information and report it to the appropriate audience, i.e., the audience(s) who will make and implement decisions about changing implementation of the program.

 Begin your descriptions of the issues to be addressed and your primary user(s) by answering the following questions:

☐ What is the title of the program to be evaluated?

_____

_____

Throughout this chapter, this program will be referred to as the Program.

☐ What issues or key questions about the program are to be addressed by the evaluation?

_____

_____

☐ Who needs to be involved in the evaluation? Who will make decisions about changes? Who will implement the changes? That is, who is are the primary users? What are their key concerns about the program and any potential changes in it?

- Staff _____

  Key concerns _____

- Planners/Coordinators _____

  Key concerns _____

- Site Managers/Administrators _____

  Key concerns _____

- Local or Regional Managers _____

  Key concerns _____

- Others _____

  Key concerns _____

 Try not to serve too many audiences at once. A formative evaluation is targeted on problem solving. If too many audiences are involved, the effort may become too difficult or diffuse.

☐ Ask the people who constitute your primary users these questions:

- How would you describe the program and its objectives? _____

  _____

- What's the best source of information about the program? _____

  _____

- What do you see as its primary problem(s)?

  _____

  _____

Do some of the evaluation findings need to be used to satisfy the evaluation requirements of a funding agency or of any other group? Are specific requirements mandated? Are you required, for instance, to use particular tests to measure attainment of particular outcomes, or to report on special forms? If so, summarize these evaluation requirements by quoting or referencing the documents that stipulate them.

_____

_____

_____

_____

_____

_____

Are planning meetings regularly scheduled for the program? When are they?

_____

Is a formal report on the program due to an outside agency? If yes, when?

_____

What budget has been allocated to the evaluation? _____

Find out as much as you can about the program

Instructions

a. Collect and scrutinize written documents that describe the program.

CHECK ✓ ☐   Check whether you can obtain copies of the following:

☐ A program proposal written for the funding agency

☐ The request for proposals (RFP) written by the sponsor or funding agency to which this program's proposal was a response

☐ Results of a needs assessment whose findings the program is intended to address

☐ Written federal, state or district guidelines about program processes and goals to which this program must conform

☐ The program's budget, particularly the part that mentions the evaluation

☐ A description of, or an organizational chart depicting, the administrative, management, and staff roles played by various people in the program

☐ Guides for the materials which have been purchased for the program

☐ Past evaluations of this or similar programs

☐ Lists of goals and objectives which the staff or planners feel describe the program's aims

☐ Tests or surveys which the program planners feel may be used to measure the effects of the program, such as a districtwide year-end assessment instrument

☐ Memos, meeting minutes, newspaper articles, brochures—descriptions made by the staff or the planners of the program

☐ Descriptions of the program's history or of the social context which it has been designed to fit

☐ Articles in the professional and evaluation literature that describe the effects of programs such as the one in question, its curricular or other materials, or its various subcomponents

☐ Other_____

Once you have discovered which materials are available, seek them out and copy them if possible. Make notes in the margins. Write down or dictate onto tape comments about your general impression of the program, its context, and staff.

CHECK ✓ ☐   Find out, if possible, about these components of the program:

☐ The program's major general goals

☐ Specifically stated objectives

☐ The philosophy or point of view of the program planners

☐ Examples of similar programs that planners intend to emulate

☐ Writers in the field whose point of view the program is intended to mirror

☐ The needs of the community or constituency which the program is intended to meet—whether these have been explicitly stated or seem to implicitly underlie the program

☐ Program implementation directives and requirements

☐ The amount of variation from site to site, or even from individual to individual, that is expected by the program

☐ The number and distribution of sites involved

☐ Canned or prepublished curricula or other materials which will be used for the program

☐ Plans for materials which will be constructed in-house

☐ Plans for staff development

☐ Plans which have been developed describing how the program will look in operation—daily schedules of services, activities, scenarios, etc.

☐ Administrative, decision-making, clinical, and service roles to be played by various people

☐ Participant evaluation plans

☐ Staff evaluation plans

☐ Program evaluation plans

☐ Staff responsibilities

☐ Time lines and deadlines for accomplishing particular implementation goals or reaching certain outcomes

b. Talk to people.

Once you have arrived at a set of initial impressions, check these—and your germinating evaluation plans—by seeking out people who can give you two kinds of information:

- Advice about how to go about collecting formative information for a program of this sort

- Answers to your questions about what the program is supposed to be and do—including what and how much modification can occur based on your findings

 By all means, find the people with whom you will have the most contact and who will be in a position to use the information you collect. These people might be:

☐ The project director(s)

☐ Evaluators or consultants who have worked with the program or its staff in the past

_____

_____

☐ Staff, particularly those who seem to have most influence

_____

_____

☐ Program planners and designers

☐ Special consultants to the project

_____

_____

☐ Members of advisory committees

_____

_____

☐ Administrative personnel not directly connected with the project, but whose cooperation will help you carry out the evaluation more efficiently or quickly

☐ Influential community members

_____

_____

☐ Influential or particularly helpful participants

_____

_____

☐ The people who wrote the proposal

_____

_____

Try to think of other people involved with the program whose opinions and decisions will influence the success of the evaluation and the extent to which the information you collect will be useful and used. Make sure that you talk with each of these people, either at a group meeting or individually.

 If they are too busy to talk, send memos to key people. Describe the evaluation, what you would like them to do for you, and when.

In your meetings with these people, you should communicate two things:

- Who you are and why you are formatively evaluating the program

- The importance of your staying in contact with them throughout the course of the evaluation

They, in turn, should point out to you:

- Areas in which you have misunderstood the program's objectives or its description

- Parts of the program which will be alternatively emphasized or relatively disregarded during the term of the evaluation

- Problems they foresee in the program

- Their decision about the boundaries of the cooperation they will give you

 Keep a list of the addresses and phone numbers of the people you have contacted with notations about the best time of day to call them or the times when it is easiest for them to attend meetings.

If possible, observe the program in operation, or programs like it. Accompanied by program planners and staff, take a field trip to look at one or two similar programs. This will help the staff react to what they see. It will give you and them a better idea of what the program is supposed to look like and how it could change.

Take careful notes of everything you see and do. Later you may find some of these valuable.

Describe the program

 In this step, try to outline the distinctive features of the program. Writing this section will help you identify fuzzy areas that need clarification and also will help you rough out the introductory sections of the eventual evaluation report, should one be necessary.

 Worksheets like the following will help you organize your description of the program.

a. Fill in the worksheet on the background of the program.

CHECK ☑ ☐   **BACKGROUND WORKSHEET**

People Affected by the Program

Community

• Are special permissions needed for individuals to participate in the program? _____

• Are community members to be actively involved in the program activities? ☐

• Are they to have an advisory role? ☐

Staff

• Who are the staff for the program?
_____
_____

• What characteristics are required of staff employed, e.g., language abilities, special training or credentials, subject area skills, experience?
_____
_____
_____

• Administrators involved?
_____
_____

• Other staff?
_____
_____

• Consultants or other specialists?
_____
_____

Program Origins

• How did the program get started?
_____
_____

Was there a needs assessment? _____

• Official demands on the program

What legal or funding demands or restrictions have been placed on the program?
_____
_____

---

b. Complete the worksheet on program objectives to help you clarify what you expect to be the results or outcomes of the program.

 List the desired outcomes of the program on the worksheet below. Try to make at least one entry in each blank; this will help you think of outcomes that you might not have otherwise considered. Leave blanks empty only where you think listing outcomes would be totally irrelevant.

OBJECTIVES WORKSHEET

Desired Performance Outcomes of the Program: Cognitive and Psychomotor

- At the end of the program, the participants will have learned/changed as follows:
  _____
  _____

- At the end of the program, the staff will have learned/changed as follows:
  _____
  _____

- At the end of the program, the community members will have learned/changed as follows:
  _____
  _____

- At the end of the program, others will have learned/changed as follows:
  _____
  _____

Desired Performance Outcomes of the Program: Affective/Attitudinal

- At the end of the program, the participants will have the following attitude(s):
  _____
  _____

- At the end of the program, the staff will have the following attitude(s):
  _____
  _____

- At the end of the program, the community members will have the following attitude(s):
  _____
  _____

- At the end of the program, others will have the following attitude(s):
  _____
  _____

outcomes listed in this step to structure your meeting. Amend it according to the decisions made there. Add and subtract outcomes as necessary.

C. Fill in the Implementation Worksheet. It describes the resources, activities, services, and administrative arrangements that compose the program.

In any case, list those services and activities that you or the program planners feel are most crucial to properly carrying out the program.

 See whether you can list the most crucial activities in the program. If these lack clarity or consensus, you will need to schedule additional planning time with program designers and staff.

IMPLEMENTATION WORKSHEET

Resources

- New materials introduced for the program
  _____

- New administrative arrangements instituted in the program _____

- Equipment—projectors, laboratory equipment, etc.—purchased for the program _____

- Facilities—number of classrooms, special facilities, etc.—allotted for the program _____

- Time allotted to the program/schedule of activities
  _____
  _____

- Other _____
  _____

DECISION Do you need to meet with or poll your primary users to find out more about or to clarify program goals? Do there seem to be disagreements or inconsistencies in what constitutes the program's most important goals? If so, you will need to schedule adequate planning time to clarify these issues (see Phase B, Step 1). You may want to use the

Activities

Crucial activities, ser-vices, arrangements in Program X	A stranger who came upon the program in operation would see . . .		
	Partici-pants doing this:	Staff doing this:	Others doing this:
1.			
2.			
3.			
etc.			

Consult, as well, Chapter 5 of How to Assess Program Implementation. It lists questions to ask the staff and planners of the program to help them describe implementation.

It falls within your job role to critique the program as well as describe it and its relative effectiveness. At this point, make a judgment about the clarity and coherence of program goals and rationale. Ask yourself:

- Are the goals and objectives stated precisely enough to be understood by the program's staff and constituency?

- Or are they so unclear that they detract from the program's sense of common purpose?

- Is the rationale underpinning the program logical or well thought out?

- Or is there confusion or misunderstanding about why the program's activities should lead to its intended outcomes?

Focus the evaluation

Instructions

a. Judge the adequacy of your description of the program.

Make a note of your impressions of the quality and specificity of the program's written description. Answer these questions in particular:

- Is your description specific enough to give you a good picture of what happens in the program? Does it suggest which components you will evaluate and what they will look like?

  ☐ yes   ☐ no   ☐ uncertain

- Have program planners written a clear rationale describing why the particular activities, processes, materials, and administrative arrangements in the program will lead to the goals and objectives specified for the program?

  ☐ yes   ☐ no   ☐ uncertain

- Is the program that is planned, and/or the goals and objectives toward which it aims, consistent with the philosophy or point of view on which the program is based? Do you note misinterpretations or conflicting interpretations anywhere?

  ☐ yes   ☐ no   ☐ uncertain

If your answer to any of these questions is no or uncertain, then you will have to include in your evaluation plans discussions with the planners and staff to persuade them to set down a clear statement of the program's goals and rationale.

b. Visualize what you might do as formative evaluator.

Base this exercise upon your impressions of the program:

- Which components appear to provide the key to whether it sinks or swims? _____

- Which components do the planners and staff most emphasize as being critically important? _____

- Which are likely to fail? Why? _____

- What might be missing from the program as planned that could turn out to be critical for its success? _____

- Where is the program too poorly planned to merit success? _____

- Which program outcomes will probably be easiest to accomplish? Which will be most difficult? _____

- What effects might the program have that its planners have not anticipated? _____

While conducting this exercise by yourself, do not be afraid of being hard on the program. It is your job to foresee potential problems that the program's planners might overlook.

When you think about the service you can provide, you, of course, will need to consider two important things besides program characteristics and outcomes. These are the budget, which you inquired about in Step 1, and your own particular strengths and talents.

C. Assess your own strengths.

 You will best benefit the program in those areas where your visualization in Step **3b** matches your expertise. You should "tune" the evaluation to build on your skills as:

☐ A researcher

☐ A group process leader or organizational facilitator

☐ A subject matter "expert"—perhaps a curriculum designer

☐ A program designer

☐ An administrator/manager

☐ A facilitator for problem solving

☐ A synthesizer or conceptualizer

☐ A disseminator of information, or public relations promoter

☐ Other _____

Chapter 2 presented a general outline of the tasks that often fall within the formative evaluator's role. You will have to work out your own job with your own evaluation sponsor and users. Meet again and confer with the people whose cooperation will be necessary—those whose decisions about the program carry most influence and who will cooperate when you gather information. You may, of course, also want to meet with other audiences.

a. Agree about the basic outline of the evaluation.

☐ Agree about the program characteristics and outcomes that will be your major focus—regardless of the prominence given them in official descriptions. Ask the planners and staff these questions:

- Which characteristics of the program do you consider most important for accomplishing its objectives? Might you have implemented it in a different way than is currently planned? Would you be willing to undertake a planned variation study and try this other way?

_____

_____

- Are there particularly expensive, troublesome, controversial, or difficult-to-implement parts of the program that you might like to change or eliminate? Could we conduct some pilot or feasibility studies, altering these on a trial basis at some sites?

_____

_____

- Are there components you would like the program to have which do not currently exist? Might we try some of these on a pilot basis?

_____

_____

- Which outcomes are of highest priority?

_____

_____

- On which outcomes do you expect the program to have most direct and easily observed effect?

_____

_____

- Does the program have social or political objectives that should be monitored? _____

_____

See How to Focus an Evaluation, Chapter 4, for additional help with narrowing the focus to a reasonable set of expectations.

☐ Agree about the sites and people from whom you will collect information. Ask these questions:

- At which sites will the program be in operation? How geographically dispersed are they?

_____

_____

- How much does the program as implemented vary from site to site? Where can such variations be seen?

_____

_____

- Who are the important people to talk with and observe? _____

_____

- When are the most critical times to see the program—occasions over its duration, and also hours during the day? _____

_____

• At what points during the course of the program will it be best to assess participant progress, staff attitudes, etc.? Are there logical breaking points at, say, the completion of particular key units or semesters? Or does the program progress steadily, or each participant individually, with no best time to assess or observe? _____

_____

• Would it be better to monitor the program as a whole periodically, or should the effectiveness of various program subparts be singled out for scrutiny, or both? _____

_____

 More detailed description of sampling plans is contained in How to Assess Program Implementation, pages 49 to 53, and How to Use Qualitative Methods in Evaluation, pages 51 to 60. How to Design a Program Evaluation, pages 35 to 48, describes decisions you might make about when to make measurements.

☐ Agree about the part the staff will play in collecting, sharing, and providing information. Explain to the staff that its cooperation will allow you to collect richer and more credible information about the program—with a clearer message about what needs to be done. Ask these questions:

• Can records kept during the program as a matter of course be collected or copied to provide information for the evaluation? _____

_____

• Can record-keeping systems be established to give me needed information? _____

_____

• Will you—staff and others—be able to share achievement or performance information with me or help with its collection? Are you willing to administer periodic assessments to samples of participants?

_____

• Will staff members be willing and able to attend brief evaluation meetings or evaluation planning sessions?

_____

• Will you be willing and able to take part in planned program variations or pilot tests? Will you be willing to respond to attitude surveys to determine the effectiveness of program components?

_____

_____

• Based on the information I collect, will you be willing to spend time on modifying the program through new activities, schedules, organizational, or staffing patterns? _____

_____

• Are you willing to adopt a formative wait-and-see experimental attitude toward the program?

_____

_____

 How to Assess Program Implementation describes ways to use records kept during the program to assess program implementation and outcomes (see pages 60 to 71).

☐ Agree about the extent to which you will be able to take a research stance toward the evaluation. Find out:

• Will it be possible to set up control groups with whom program progress can be compared?

_____

_____

• Will it be possible to establish a true control group design by randomly assigning participants to different variations of the program or to a no-program control group? Will it be possible to delay introducing the program at some sites?

_____

_____

• Can non-equivalent control groups be formed or located? _____

_____

• Will I have a chance to make assessments or collect observations prior to the program and/or often enough to set up a time series design?

_____

_____

• Will I be able to use a good design to underlie pilot tests or feasibility studies?

_____

_____

• Will I be able or required to conduct in-depth case studies at some sites?

_____

_____

Details about the use of designs in formative evaluation are discussed in How to Design a Program Evaluation. See in particular pages 14 to 20 and 20 to 23. Case studies are discussed in How to Assess Program Implementation, pages 30 to 33, and in How to Use Qualitative Methods in Evaluation.

☐ Agree about the extent to which you will need to provide other services. Ask the staff and planners these questions:

- Do you need consultative help that stretches my role beyond collecting formative data? Do you want my advice about program modifications, for instance? Or help with solving personnel problems?

- Do you want me to serve to some degree as a linking agent? Should I, for instance, conduct literature reviews, seek consultation from similar projects, or search out services or additional people or funds to help the project?

- Should I take on a public relations role? Will you want me to serve as a spokesperson for the project? To give talks or write a newsletter, for example?

b. Stay alert for two potential snags in carrying out the evaluation.

- Lack of possibilities for changing the program

- Conflicts in your own responsibilities to the program and the sponsor

☐ Look out for lack of commitment to change on the part of planners or staff. It will be fruitless to collect data to modify the program if modifications are likely to be resisted. Before you begin scrutinizing the program or its various components, then, you should find out where funding requirements, staff opinion, or the political surroundings restrict alterations of the program. Ask in particular the following questions:

- On what are you most and least willing, or constrained, to spend additional money? What materials, personnel, or facilities?

- Where would you be most agreeable to cutbacks? Can you, for instance, remove personnel? If

particular program components were found to be ineffective, would you eliminate them? Which services, materials, and other program activities would you be willing to delete?

- Would you be willing to scrap the program as it currently looks and start over?

- How much administrative or staff reorganization will you tolerate? Can you change people's roles? Can you add to staff, say, by bringing in volunteers? Can you move people—staff, clients, other participants—from location to location permanently or temporarily? Can you reassign individuals to different programs or groups?

- How much programmatic change will you tolerate in the program beyond its current state? Would you be willing to delete, add, or alter the program's objectives? To what extent would you be willing to change materials and other program components? Are you willing to redesign activities?

Include additional "what if . . . " questions that are more specific to the program at hand.

☐ Look out for conflicts in your own role. If your job requires that you report about the program to its sponsor or to the community at large, staff members are likely to be reluctant to share with you doubts and conjectures about the program. Since this will hamper your effectiveness, you will do best to explain to the planners and staff the following:

- That you do not intend to write a summative report that judges and finds fault with the program. Outline the form and some of the message that the report will contain.

  and/or

- That the planners and staff will have a chance to review reports that you submit to the sponsor.

  and/or

- That you are willing to write a final report describing only those aspects of the program chosen by the staff.

  and/or

- That you are willing to swear confidentiality about the issues and activities (or some sensitive subsection of them) that the formative evaluation addresses.

Come to preliminary agreement about services and responsibilities

---

Instructions

Before you launch into an intensive and detailed planning effort in Phase B, you will want to agree on the general outline of services you intend to provide and the minimum budget that will be available to you. You will enter into a more detailed contract agreement at the end of Phase B.

 You may want to document this agreement in the form of a memo to the sponsor.

NOTE If you anticipate needing to spend extended time in planning meetings with staff to help them clarify the goals, rationale, and activities of the program, then you may want to enter into a formal contractual agreement for this part of your service now. Since the evaluation costs for this type of planning will mostly be in your time, you can estimate the costs fairly easily. See Phase B, Step 7 for advice on how to estimate the costs of staff time, and Step 8 for guidelines for constructing a formal agreement.

Your agreement at this point should cover:

☐ The purpose of the evaluation

☐ The general approach you plan to use (what you plan to examine and how you'll do it)

- Attention to program description/articulation, i.e., clarifying the goals and objectives of the program, its principal activities, organizational arrangements, roles and responsibilities, and the rationale underlying presumed relationships between program operations and outcomes

  _____

  _____

- The program components, activities, arrangements, etc. you plan to examine. (If you don't yet know which ones, describe the process and criteria you'll use in your selection process.)

  _____

  _____

- The program outcomes you will monitor. (If you don't yet know which ones, describe the process and criteria you'll use in your selection process.)

  _____

- Participant and staff characteristics you'll be interested in _____

- Context data and other factors you'll consider

  _____

  _____

- Data collection methods you plan to utilize (e.g., tests, observations, interviews, questionnaires)

  _____

☐ Meeting and reporting schedule

☐ Any assumptions you have about staff and other resources that will be available to you from the program (e.g., program records, staff time to administer instruments, random assignment options, feasibility/pilot test options)

☐ Budget available

NOTE Don't become too detailed at this point as you will want to leave yourself as much flexibility as possible for Phase B planning with staff. Consider this agreement as a statement of the minimum you will provide, stated at a level of generality that retains some options.

 NOTE If you are in a hurry, and you think you need to purchase instruments for the evaluation, then get started on this right away. Consult Phase B, Step 7 and Phase C, Step 1 as well as the relevant How to books and order specimen sets as soon as possible.

Select Appropriate Evaluation Methods

Instructions

=====

The first step of Phase B may not be necessary if the program has been thoughtfully and specifically planned and/or is based on adapting a canned program to the setting. On the other hand, if planners are building a program de novo, then you may have to devote considerable attention to this, describing and justifying the program prior to planning suitable evaluation methods.

Phase B has eight steps:

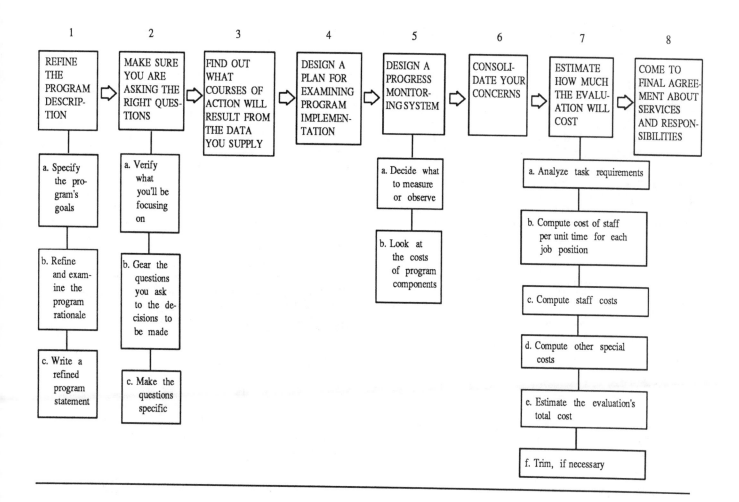

1	2	3	4	5	6	7	8
REFINE THE PROGRAM DESCRIPTION	MAKE SURE YOU ARE ASKING THE RIGHT QUESTIONS	FIND OUT WHAT COURSES OF ACTION WILL RESULT FROM THE DATA YOU SUPPLY	DESIGN A PLAN FOR EXAMINING PROGRAM IMPLEMENTATION	DESIGN A PROGRESS MONITORING SYSTEM	CONSOLIDATE YOUR CONCERNS	ESTIMATE HOW MUCH THE EVALUATION WILL COST	COME TO FINAL AGREEMENT ABOUT SERVICES AND RESPONSIBILITIES

1.
a. Specify the program's goals
b. Refine and examine the program rationale
c. Write a refined program statement

2.
a. Verify what you'll be focusing on
b. Gear the questions you ask to the decisions to be made
c. Make the questions specific

5.
a. Decide what to measure or observe
b. Look at the costs of program components

7.
a. Analyze task requirements
b. Compute cost of staff per unit time for each job position
c. Compute staff costs
d. Compute other special costs
e. Estimate the evaluation's total cost
f. Trim, if necessary

Refine the program description

In Phase A, Steps 2 and 3, you described the program as best you could and then decided whether there was sufficient agreement and clarity about program goals and arrangements to ground your evaluation. If your decision was negative, you were advised to schedule time with planners and staff to refine program plans. Now is the time.

a. Specify the program's goals.

Meet again with the program staff to persuade them to express the outcome and implementation goals of their program in observable terms. This will no doubt require more than rewording. It might even be necessary for the staff to select whole new sets of goals and objectives which are prerequisite to accomplishing the goals they have outlined.

 Use the worksheets you developed in Phase A, Step 3 to help structure your meeting. Ask staff and planners such questions as "What do you expect participants to be able to do after the program? How will they be different? How do you want them to change as a result of the program?"

 Describe the goals and objectives of the program to which you think your evaluation will need to most closely attend, and ask the staff and planners to react to your list, adding, deleting, or modifying as they see fit.

 Then list program goals according to priority.

Cognitive or performance goals:

_____

_____

Attitude goals: _____

_____

Other goals—for instance, organizational, political, community focused: _____

_____

 To help people to be more clear about what implementation of the program should look like, have staff and planners complete this table:

| Crucial activities, services and components in the program | A stranger who came upon the activity or component in operation would see . . . | | | Because |
	Participants doing this:	Staff doing this:	Others doing this:	
1. 2. 3. etc.				

 Consult, as well, Chapter 2 of How to Assess Program Implementation. It lists questions to ask the staff to help them describe program implementation in detail.

 Then list the major characteristics of program implementation:

_____

_____

 While you are talking to people, put together, as well, preliminary plans about how you will assess goal attainment.

Say to the planners and staff members:

Now that you've stated a goal or an objective of the program, what evidence would convince you that participants have met the goal or mastered the objective? What will this look like in present learning or performance? How will this look in future performance? What present performance would satisfy you that there is good progress toward the objective?

What evidence would convince you that the future performance is likely to come about?

Ask them to consider as well:

• What evidence would convince you that individuals are not attaining the goals that you have set?

• How much of this negative evidence would it take for you to decide that the program is not accomplishing what you intended?

These are, of course, hard questions; but their answers will determine the direction of your data collection plans.

b. Refine and examine the program rationale.

The goal of this step is to help the people who planned the program think through the program rationale, or theory, on which the program rests. This theory should be consistent and clear enough to be understood by everyone working in the program or evaluating it.

 Consult How to Assess Program Implementation, pages 29 to 32, for a discussion of evaluations based on theories of learning or behavior, principles of organization, or other theoretical models.

Like Step 1a, this step should take place in consultation with program planners and staff—the key people you identified and contacted in Phase A.

The extent to which you are able to sketch out and examine the rationale underlying the program will depend on your skills as a questioner. This step demands that the program staff scrutinize its own thinking about the likelihood that the program it has planned will bring about its objectives.

Based on your own reading and discussion about the program and the notes you took in Steps 2 and 3 of Phase A, you probably have a good idea of areas where the planners have not adequately linked the program's characteristics and processes with its intended goals. Try to focus the meeting on any "loose ends"—planned activities that do not appear to advance the stated goals, as well as goals that are not sufficiently addressed by planned activities.

If people are likely to be defensive about the plans they have already made for a program, this may be a difficult step to complete satisfactorily. If you feel that you lack the skill to involve the staff in this sort of serious thinking, discuss the need for activities of this sort with the project director and try to enlist his or her help. Perhaps the director can hold a workshop or a consultant can be brought in.

 However it is developed, the program rationale should attend to these topics:

☐ The activities, arrangements, materials, and organization of staff roles that compose the program, with an explanation of why each is expected to lead directly or indirectly to attainment of the program objectives. These explanations could take the form of chains of events: "Participants do _____, which leads to _____, which helps them to learn _____, which helps them to achieve _____, or to believe _____."

☐ The length of time it should take for participants to reach major objectives.

☐ The amount of time per day or week which will be allocated to experience with program activities that are considered crucial for achieving major outcomes, and an assessment of the adequacy of this amount of time for producing them.

☐ A description of provisions which have been made to motivate people to work with and follow through with these activities for the amounts of time or in the manner prescribed.

 These hard questions should be answered as specifically as possible. Few programs as initially planned attend to these critical program features in realistic enough detail.

c. Write a refined program statement.

The refined statement is an in-house report, to be shared among staff members and evaluators, in which you record what you have learned about the major goals of the program as well as why and when the program is expected to achieve them. The program statement should be used as a guide for your evaluation and as a description of the program for anyone who is interested.

 How to Assess Program Implementation, Chapter 7, outlines an implementation report and the Appendix details the specific questions that may be addressed. The questions filling each section of the outline show the level of detail that the program statement should use to describe the program.

Try to summarize the program's major activities, services, and materials, and their rationale in a table such as the following:

Table for Describing Intended Program Implementation

Program Component:

Outcome objective addressed	Target group	Principal activities or services to be provided	Staffing	Special resources or materials	Special location or organiza- tional contact	Frequency or duration	Amount of progress expected	Person responsible for imple- mentation

 As the program changes and develops, you will need periodically to alter the program statement. Sometimes modifying the statement might seem an extraneous activity; but if the staff is at all interested in disseminating or enlarging the program, or announcing its benefits to the community, the program statement will serve as a constantly useful source of what to tell people.

In the previous step and/or in Phase A you described program outcomes, activities, and rationale.

This description offers a wealth of evaluation possibilities. The purpose of this step is to help you decide which outcomes and implementation aspects will be most useful for you to observe or assess. Of course, it would be nice if you could examine all activities and all outcomes. But there is probably not sufficient time and money to allow this.

Instead, you will have to shorten the list and clarify the questions you'll be addressing.

a. Verify what you'll be focusing on.

 Which outcomes? Look at the Objectives Worksheet in Phase A, Step 3b, beginning on page 51, or the goals list in Phase B, Step 1a. For now, simply circle those that are perceived as the most important, the ones you agreed to monitor in Phase A, Step 6, plus others that might now interest you for other reasons.

 Which aspects of program implementation? Your agreement in Phase A, Step 6 lists the program activities/components you planned to examine, and additional potential problem areas may have emerged during your program description activities in Phase B, Step 1. List those that now appear most in need of your attention. Verify your impressions with those of planners and staff.

b. Gear the questions you ask to the decisions to be made.

Having decided on components and outcomes, you now need to agree on the quesions which will guide your monitoring activities. These questions should reflect the decisions the program planners and staff want to make about each component.

These questions will usually take one of several forms:

• What does Component X look like—so that it can be described?

• To what extent does Component X operate smoothly and as it is supposed to—so that problem areas can be modified?

• To what extent does Component X achieve its objectives? So that weaknesses can be corrected?

• Is Component X worth keeping as is?

 Write down the question(s) you want to answer about each program component you have agreed to examine:

_____

_____

_____

_____

 The answers to questions about what the program looks like lie in studies of program implementation. How to Assess Program Implementation, Chapter 2, contains a set of questions to help you decide how much backup data you will have to collect to support your description of the program's implementation. How to Use Qualitative Methods in Evaluation explains the design and use of less structured interview and observation techniques.

 Answers to questions about whether a component should be changed or kept as is will lie in your implementation findings and in measures of progress toward objectives. Specifying objectives and questions for these latter purposes is discussed in How to Measure Attitudes and in How to Measure Performance.

If the issue is whether or not to keep a particular component, then write a question to that effect. For example, "Are the home visits worth keeping or should they be changed or discarded?"

c. Make the questions specific.

Once you have outlined important questions, you need to make them specific enough to focus the assessments, observations, and comparisons to be made. Scrutinize each question and think of how you can ask it more specifically. A question, "Is the counseling component worth it?" might be further specified like this:

What does "worth it" mean? For the purpose of evaluation, it means:

- Students perceive it as helpful
- Teachers think it beneficial
- Students follow up on suggested referrals
- Students make progress with their problems

As another, more general example, "Is program component X working smoothly and as intended?" might be further specified to mean:

- The community is aware of the service
- Staff members are clear on required procedures
- Client treatment plans are individualized

- Expectations for clients are clear and explicit
- Parents are involved in the treatment
- Most clients complete their treatment plan
- Staff receive adequate support in terms of training, monitoring, leadership, etc.
- Interactions between and among staff, administrators, and clients are productive.

Check these questions with the staff to make sure that your data collection plan addresses their concerns and the problems they perceive. Refine questions accordingly. Sometimes the staff is unable to articulate clearly their specific concerns and often refining understandings of problems and of the specific issues which underlie them is an important outcome of the evaluation process itself.

Step 3

Find out what courses of action will result from the data you supply

---

Instructions

If your job is to collect information that will be used for deciding whether to change, keep, or drop a program component, then find out from the staff the most likely course of action they will take if the component proves unsatisfactory so that you can build into the evaluation a plan to assess the likely merits of this option as well.

For each component you examine, have the staff complete this statement:

"If the _____ component turns out to be unsatisfactory, we will do _____ instead."

Whatever is entered in the second blank defines what comparison groups should experience.

Design a plan for examining program implementation

Instructions

This step has to do with finding ways to get credible information to answer the staff's questions about what the program, and its various planned or natural variations, look like and where problems may be arising. Your information-gathering plan will have two major components:

- A set of data collection techniques and/or instruments which you have chosen to use for answering critical

  questions. Choice of procedures can be facilitated by reading How to Assess Program Implementation and How to Use Qualitative Methods in Evaluation.

- A sampling plan or an evaluation design which prescribes when specific evaluation procedures or instruments will be implemented, the sites at which this will take place, and the people, classes, groups, or locations who will be the

  focus of activity. How to Design a Program Evaluation, will help you select an appropriate quantitative design. How to Assess Program Implementation, Chapter 3, describes sampling considerations for choosing sites, times to measure, and events to observe. How to Use Qualitative Methods in Evaluation, Chapter 3, describes sampling and design considerations for conducting case studies.

Summarize your data collection plans for describing implementation in a table like the following:

Once you have read through How to Assess Program Implementation and How to Use Qualitative Methods in Evaluation, or otherwise made a decision about which instruments and techniques you will use to examine each component, list them—questionnaires, interviews, observations, examination of program or management information system records—in Column 2 of the table. (In Column 1, just briefly note the name of the program component—activity, service, organizational arrangement, or set of materials—you will examine.) If it's at all possible, try to use more than one data source or instrument for examining each aspect.

In Column 3, list the dates when data will be collected or observations conducted. In Column 4, list the sites which you have chosen to examine. Choice of sites depends on the questions you are attempting to answer. If the program is known to vary considerably from site to site, include representatives of each version of the program in your selection. This will be particularly crucial if you are exploring the relative effects of different planned or natural variations in the program. If the program is intended to be uniform across sites, choose sites based on other criteria such as the length of time the program has been in operation at the site, the amount of experience of staff, the characteristics of the neighborhoods involved, the amount of funds allotted to the program, or relative effectiveness. Choose as many sites as your budget will endure.

In Column 5 of the table—subjects—name the groups on whom you will focus for each procedure (staff, community members, participants, parents, etc.) and how you will sample them, if necessary, for your study.

Table for Summarizing a Program Monitoring Plan

1 Activity/component to be examined	2 Data collection techniques or instrument selected	3 Dates of data collection	4 Sites to be examined	5 Subjects
Group therapy	Participant interviews Staff questionnaires Attendance records Session observations	Oct. 1-31	2 most effective 2 least effective	20% random sample of participants All staff

On a separate sheet, record the names and addresses, if necessary, of people you will need to contact in order to collect your data. Once you have mapped out your general plan for implementation data, go on to specify a similar plan for assessing performance, attitudes, and costs.

 If there is to be a control group, construct a data collection plan for describing what occurs to it while the program group is taking part in the program. If the control group is to receive no program, plan to verify that this is the case. If the control group is receiving a program or a component that represents an alternative the staff might adopt, then you should monitor the control group's program as carefully as that of the program group.

Design a progress monitoring system

---

a. Decide what to measure or observe.

Chapter 2 of this handbook, pages 26 to 41, offers some rules-of-thumb for deciding which kinds of assessments might be most useful to the planners and staff.

For the purpose of monitoring program progress in performance or attitude outcomes, try to locate already existing instruments rather than spend time constructing them from scratch. Unless your questions are so program-specific that you will not be able to find already developed measures, investigate what is available. Investigate also data which may already be available and accessible through existing management information systems.

The books How to Measure Performance and How to Measure Attitudes suggest myriad sources of already existing instruments. You might consider as well tests and questionnaires that have accompanied the program's materials, if such things exist.

If you have chosen not to purchase or borrow an instrument, then How to Measure Attitudes and How to Measure Performance instruct you in the design of instruments that will be useful for collecting information.

For monitoring progress, you will want tests or other measures that give as specific information as possible. Where possible, select measures that yield subscales to help you determine the strengths and gaps in achievement/performance.

b. Look at the costs of program components if a critical factor determining the choice among program activities or indicating their relative worth is the costs they incur.

Sometimes a program component that seems to be effective might still be considered undesirable because of the large amount of money involved in purchasing or maintaining it. For formative evaluation, assess costs by keeping track of

the expenses demanded for each component's continued implementation over one program cycle, say, a year. Add up, therefore:

Initial cost of materials	$_____
Cost of maintenance and repair	_____
Cost of training staff	_____
Cost of staff time spent implementing the component	_____
TOTAL	$_____

c. Once you have chosen the instruments you will acquire or construct for assessing the performance and cost outcomes of the program, note these on the same data collection table you used for summarizing your implementation data plan in Step 4. Column 1 in this case will reflect outcomes or costs to be monitored.

Consolidate your concerns

Using the same data collection table for both implementation and progress monitoring allows you to consolidate data collection procedures and measures. In the interest of economy of time and money, and so that your evaluation is not intrusive on the program, try to administer within any data collection period only one instrument of a particular type—questionnaire, interview, achievement test, etc.—to each group of people or individuals from whom you will gather information. Do not give staff a questionnaire about program implementation and a questionnaire assessing their attitudes. Pool all these questions into a single instrument. The following table can help you consolidate:

1 Instrument	2 Program implementation outcome questions to be addressed	3 Date(s) of administration	4 Sites to be examined	5 Subjects to be sampled
Staff questionnaire	Logistics of new attendance policy Perceptions of its affect on student performance Attitude toward district management and support Frequency of student referrals			
Administrator interview				
etc.				

List in Column 1 the data collection techniques and instruments that will be administered to examine program implementation and/or to monitor progress in performance or changes in attitudes. In Column 2, briefly note which activity or cognitive/affective outcome will be monitored and

the specific questions to be addressed. In Column 3, list dates when instruments will be administered. In Column 4, record the sites chosen for each data-gathering date; and in Column 5, list the people from whom data will be collected, or who will be observed.

If there is a control group, list in Columns 3, 4, and 5 the dates, places, and people relevant to examining the control group's program and progress.

Instructions

If the project intends to pay for your services, you will have to determine early the financial bounds that constrain the evaluation.

The cost of an evaluation is difficult to predict accurately. This is unfortunate, since what you will be able to promise the staff and planners will be determined by what you feel you can afford to do.

Estimate costs by getting the easy ones out of the way first. Find out costs per unit for each of these "fixed" expenses:

- ☐ Postage and shipping (bulk rate, parcel post, etc.) _____
- ☐ Photocopying and printing _____
- ☐ Travel and transportation _____
- ☐ Long-distance phone calls _____
- ☐ Test and instrument purchase _____
- ☐ Consultants _____
- ☐ Mechanical test or questionnaire scoring _____
- ☐ Data processing _____

These fixed costs will come "off the top" each time you sketch out the budget accompanying an alternative method for evaluating the program.

The most difficult cost to estimate is the most important one: the price of person-hours required for your services and those of the staff you assemble for the evaluation. If you are inexperienced, try to emulate other people. Ask how other evaluators estimate costs and then do likewise.

Develop a rule-of-thumb that computes the cost of each type of evaluation staff member per unit time period, such as "It costs $6,000 for one senior evaluator, working full time, per month." This figure should summarize all expenses of the evaluation, excluding only overhead and costs unique to a particular study, such as travel and data analysis.

The staff cost per unit should include:

Salary of a staff member for that time unit

+ Benefits

+ Office and equipment rental

+ Secretarial and support services

+ Photocopying and duplicating

+ Telephones

+ Utilities

→ This equals the total routine expenses of running your office for the time unit in question, divided by the number of full-time evaluators working there.

Compute such a figure for each salary classification—Ph.D.'s, master's level staff, data gatherers, etc. Since the cost of each of these staff positions will differ, you can plan variously priced evaluations by juggling amounts of time to be spent on the evaluation by staff members in different salary brackets.

The tasks you promise to perform in turn will determine and be determined by the amount of time you can allot to the evaluation from different staff levels. A formative evaluation will cost more if it requires the attention of the most skilled and highly priced evaluators on your staff, with repeated feedback to staff, and possibly pilot studies, than if it simply establishes an overall monitoring system where graduate students or staff routinely collect data.

 To estimate the cost of your evaluation, try these steps:

a. Do a task analysis of the tasks and resources required to complete your evaluation. Designate who is to be involved in each task and the amount of time required. Use a chart such as the one on the following page.

Task Analysis for Costing

| | Personnel Time Required (In hours or days) | | | | Other Special Costs (Service or materials purchased, travel, consultants, specialists, printing, mailing or communication) |
	Senior	Associate	Junior	Clerical/ Secretarial	

General Planning
Instrument Development
  Critical Thinking Test
    Specification
      Item Development
      Item Try-out
    . . .
 	
  Staff Questionnaire
    . . .
 	
Data Collection
  Critical Thinking Test
  Staff Questionnaire
 	
Data Analysis
  Critical Thinking Test
  Staff Questionnaire
    . . .
  Relationship between
  instruments
 	
Reporting
 	
TOTALS					

GO BACK

To complete this task analysis, go back to the schedule you developed in Step 6.

b. Compute a cost-of-staff-per-unit-time figure for each job position occupied by someone who will work on the evaluation.

Depending on the amount of overhead staff support entered into the equation, this figure could be as high as twice the gross salary earned by a person in that position.

c. Compute the staff costs of the project by multiplying the cost-of-staff-per-unit-time figure by the total time estimated by Step **a** for each job position.

d. Compute the other special costs associated with the project.

The special costs will vary depending on the specific requirements of the project. These include such things as travel for data collection, test purchase or duplication, data coding services, computer services, mailing or shipping costs associated with data collection, consultant costs. The worksheets on the following pages may help you with your estimate.

Estimated Travel Costs

Task #	Destination/ Purpose	No. of People	No. of Trips	No. of Days	Air Fare	Ground Transportation	Per Diem Hotel & Meals	TOTAL
3	Data Collection	3	4	2	$200 x 3 people x 4 trips = 2400	$50 x 3 people x 4 trips = 600	$90 x 3 people x 2 days x 4 trips = 2160	5160
							TOTAL: $_____	

Estimated Consultant Costs

Task #	Consultant	Daily Fee	No. of Days	Total Fee	Travel Costs			TOTAL
					Air Fare	Ground Transp.	Per Diem	
5	Data Analyst	200	5	1000	500	50	3 x $90 = 270	1820
							TOTAL: $_____	

Other Special Costs

Special Printing:*

_____ Surveys x _____ pages each x # needed
x $.__/page = _____

_____ Final Reports x _____ pages each
x # copies = _____

Materials Purchase

_____ Tests x $.__/each = _____

Mail:*

Mailing and return of surveys and other instruments
packages x _____ cost average each way
x 2 = _____

Phone:

Long-distance calls for telephone surveys
_____ calls x $___ per call = _____

Computer

Data entry _____
Computer time _____

*Be sure to include the extras you'll need for data collection
follow-ups.

☐ Employing junior staff members for some of the
design, data-gathering, and report writing tasks

☐ Finding volunteer help, perhaps by persuading the staff
that you can supply richer and more varied information
or reach more sites if you have their cooperation

☐ Purchasing measures rather than designing your own

☐ Cutting planning time by building the evaluation on
procedures that you, or people whose expertise you can
easily tap, have used before

☐ Consolidating instruments and the times of their
administration

☐ Planning to look at different sites with different degrees
of thoroughness, concentrating your efforts on those
factors of greatest importance

☐ Using paper-and-pencil instruments that can be machine
read and scored, where possible

☐ Relying more heavily on information that will be
collected by others, such as state-administered tests,
and records that are part of the program

e. Estimate the evaluation's total cost.

Total the costs estimated in c and d above. Add also your
indirect or overhead costs, if any. Compare this figure with
the amount you know to be already earmarked for the
evaluation. If your budget is too high, consider whether
funders may be persuaded to increase the funding.

f. Trim, if necessary.

 See if one or more of the following
strategies will reduce your requirement for
expensive personnel time, or trim some of
the fixed costs:

☐ Sampling. Rather than visiting an entire population of
program sites, for instance, visit a small sample of
them, perhaps one-third. Send observers with checklists to a slightly larger sample, and perhaps send
questionnaires to the whole group of sites to corroborate the findings from the visits and observations.

Come to final agreement about services and responsibilities

A formal agreement outlining the duties of the formative evaluator and the program staff could conform to the following format:

This agreement, made on _____, 19__ , outlines the formative evaluation of the _____ project, funded by _____ for the year _____ to _____. The evaluation will take place from _____, 19__ to _____, 19__. The formative evaluator for this project is _____ assisted by _____ and _____.

Focus of the Evaluation

Evaluation plans have been developed in collaboration with project planners and staff. All parties agree to the need for the following evaluation activities:

The formative evaluator will examine the implementation of the following program characteristics and components across all sites: _____

_____

Implementation of the following planned or natural program variations will be monitored as well:

_____

_____

The evaluator also will examine progress in the achievement of these cognitive, attitudinal, performance, and/or other outcomes: _____

_____

The evaluator, in addition, will conduct feasibility and pilot studies to answer the following questions:

_____

_____

The evaluator will provide, as well, the following services to the staff and planners:

_____

_____

Data Collection Plans

Program Monitoring

Data collection for ongoing monitoring of implementation and progress toward objectives will take place during the following periods: from _____ to _____; from _____ to _____; and from _____ to _____. These dates were chosen because _____.

Interim reports, delivered to _____ and to _____, will be due on _____, 19__, _____, 19__, _____, 19__, and _____, 19__.

Approximately _____ sites for collection of implementation data will be chosen on a _____ (random/ volunteer) basis. Of these, _____ will be studied intensively using a case study method; _____ will be examined by means of observation and interviews; and _____ will receive questionnaires or have records reviewed only. Staff members filling the following roles will be asked to cooperate: _____

_____

Approximately _____ sites will take part in each assessment of progress toward program outcomes. These will be chosen on a _____ basis. Within each of these sites, subjects will be chosen as follows:

_____

_____

During each assessment period listed above, the following types of instruments will be administered:

_____

_____

Pilot and Feasibility Studies

Pilot and feasibility studies will be conducted at approximately _____ sites, chosen on a _____ basis. The purpose and probable duration of each study is outlined below: _____

_____

Tentative completion dates for these studies are
_____, 19___, _____, 19___, and _____, 19___,
with reports delivered to _____ and _____ on
_____, 19___, _____, 19___, and _____, 19___.

The following implementation, attitude, achievement, and
other instruments will be constructed for data collection:

Staff Participation

Staff members have agreed to cooperate with and assist
data collection during monitoring, testing, and pilot
studies in the following ways:

Approximately _____ meetings will be needed to report
and describe the evaluation's findings. These meetings,
scheduled to occur a few days after submission of interim
reports, will be attended by people filling the following
roles: _____

_____

The planners and staff have agreed that decisions such
as the following might result from the formative evaluation:

_____

_____

Budget

The evaluation as planned is anticipated to require the
following expenditures:

Direct Salaries	$_____
Evaluation and Assistant Benefits	$_____
Other Direct Costs:	
Supplies and materials	$_____
Travel	$_____
Consultant services	$_____
Equipment rental	$_____
Communication	$_____
Printing and duplicating	$_____
Data processing	$_____
Equipment purchase	$_____
Facility rental	$_____
Total Direct Costs	$_____
Indirect Costs	$_____
TOTAL COSTS	$_____

Variance Clause

The staff and planners of the _____ program, and the
evaluator, agree that the evaluation outlined here represents an approximation of the formative services to be
delivered during the period _____, 19___ to _____,
19___.

Since both the program and the evaluation are likely to
change, however, all parties agree that aspects of the
evaluation can be negotiated.

The contract outlined here prescribes the evaluation's general
outline only. If you plan to describe either the program or
the evaluation in greater detail, then include tables such as
those developed in Steps 6 and 7.

Collect and Analyze Information

At this point, the program evaluation has been thoroughly planned and is getting underway. The purpose of Phase C is to help you through the process of data collection and analysis. By this time, what remains is to see that everything proceeds as expected.

The steps in Phase C can be summarized as follows:

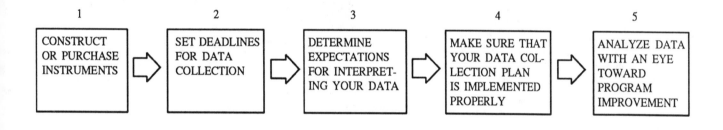

1	2	3	4	5
CONSTRUCT OR PURCHASE INSTRUMENTS	SET DEADLINES FOR DATA COLLECTION	DETERMINE EXPECTATIONS FOR INTERPRETING YOUR DATA	MAKE SURE THAT YOUR DATA COLLECTION PLAN IS IMPLEMENTED PROPERLY	ANALYZE DATA WITH AN EYE TOWARD PROGRAM IMPROVEMENT

Construct or purchase instruments

Instructions

Build a schedule for developing or obtaining any necessary instruments using the table below.

In Column 1 of the table, name each instrument or data collection method to be used. In Column 2, indicate whether it is to be made in-house or purchase, and from where. Name in Column 3 the person responsible for securing each instrument. In Column 4, remind yourself of when it is to be used. Column 5 shows the deadline—a date at least two weeks before its planned administration—for receipt of the completed instrument. If you will have to train observers or administrators to use the instrument, then set this date at least a month prior to its administration.

With regard to the Production/Receipt Deadline, Column 5, make sure that you schedule receipt of the instrument at least a week to 10 days before the administration deadline. This should allow for delays without seriously jeopardizing the rest of your schedule. Remember that constructing a test, questionnaire, interview, or observation schedule generally requires several drafts and tryouts.

Leave sufficient time for planners and staff members to review any instruments you develop. Consider involving them in the development process.

Instrument Acquisition Table

1	2	3	4	5
Description of data collection technique or name of instrument	To be developed or purchased (where)?	Person responsible for development or ordering	Date(s) of data collection	Date instrument must be produced or received

Set deadlines for data collection

Instructions

Building on the table you developed in Step 1, the following table should help you schedule and keep track of data collection activities and ensure their timely completion.

Each of the How to books in the *Program Evaluation Kit* contains suggestions for implementing the data collection techniques and instruments you are using as well as detailed directions for recording, scoring, and summarizing their results.

Assign responsibilities and fill in deadlines for each phase of each instrument's use:

- Date by which instruments must be produced or received from publisher

- Who is responsible for data collection (sending out instruments and ensuring their return, or conducting observations, interviews, etc.)

- Whether training is required

- Schedule of any necessary training

- Schedule for data collection

- Deadline for your receipt of data

- Deadline for scoring, coding, and/or otherwise organizing for analysis

A good rule-of-thumb to follow regarding deadlines is this:

- Start with a deadline for one of your interim reports or meetings to discuss findings and subtract at least one week. This is your latest possible deadline for having all data coded for computer analyses, recorded for hand/mechanical analyses, and/or organized for qualitative analysis—Column 8. Make the deadline earlier if you think you will need more than one week to analyze data, draw charts and graphs, and prepare your report. The timing, of course, will depend on the number of instruments and data sources you are using and the formality of your analysis and report.

If you are using surveys, allow sufficient time in your schedule for follow-up efforts—eye-catching reminders, second requests, etc.—to encourage high return rates.

Data Collection Table

1 Data collection procedure or instrument	2 Receipt or development deadline	3 Person(s) responsible for data collection	4 Training required	5 Dates of training	6 Dates of data collection and follow-up	7 Deadline for receipt of data	8 Deadline for scoring or coding

Determine expectations for interpreting your data

Instructions

Before implementing data collection, try to talk with the program planners and staff and decide how results will be interpreted. When information you collect is reported to the staff, it will need to be interpreted and acted upon. For this reason, some pre-set notion of good results will need to be established.

Ask the staff to refer to their answers to questions you asked about good and poor performance during Phase B, pp. 63-64. Then ask these questions regarding program implementation:

☐ To what extent are you willing to accept variations from the established plan?

☐ Which components or aspects of the program do you want to be implemented exactly as planned? Which will you allow to vary fairly freely?

☐ How much lapse in program schedule is acceptable?

☐ What is the minimum acceptable level of satisfaction with program processes? Or, what percentage of the participants needs to be satisfied with particular components or aspects?

Ask these questions about achievement and attitudes:

☐ What sorts of scores will indicate to you successful performance?

☐ What score distributions will indicate to you satisfactory, middling, or unsatisfactory performance? Answering this will be particularly useful. After dividing the potential score range from each instrument into appropriate categories—high, average, and poor; or mastery and non-mastery—determine the percentage of participants (or other cases) whose scores (or mean scores) should fall into the highest category and the largest tolerable percentage who can score low. Decisions to revise can be based on how closely actual performance matches these standards.

☐ If you are doing comparison testing, how much of a difference between the program and control groups will you want to see before declaring the program successful?

How to Measure Performance and Use Tests, Chapter 6, describes in greater detail interpreting test data and presenting the information to audiences for formative evaluation.

Make sure that your data collection plan is implemented properly

---

Instructions

Just as you are monitoring the program, you will need to likewise closely monitor the implementation of your data collection plans, paying attention to a myriad of tasks and details to assure the quality and timeliness of your study.

 Use the checklists below as the starting point for a master tracking schedule to help you manage the data collection process. The checklists include attention to sample selection; access to sites and respondents; instrument procurement; data collection; and data return.

Sampling Plan Checklist

1. Program sites have been selected to meet criteria consistent with study purposes. Indicate which ones:

   ☐ representative of different types of sites

   ☐ representative of different program variations

   ☐ representative of different participant characteristics

   ☐ representative of extreme cases

   ☐ representative of typical cases

   ☐ homogeneous sample

   ☐ maximum variation sample

   ☐ random sample or purposeful sample

2. List of program sites/cases selected: _____

3. List of alternate sites/cases: _____

---

4. If you are working with a control or comparison group design, list of these sites/cases:

   _____

   _____

 How to Design a Program Evaluation explains the desired characteristics of samples for implementing different quantitative designs. How to Use Qualitative Methods in Evaluation describes in more detail different types of purposeful sampling associated with qualitative designs. Note that these directions apply to selecting particular program sites for study, for selecting units or groups within a site, or for selecting individual respondents.

5. Data collection sample is consistent with study purposes and includes adequate representation of

   ☐ program components or events (which ones?)

   _____

   ☐ program roles (which ones?)

   _____

   ☐ time periods within program

   _____

   ☐ participant characteristics (name them)

   _____

   ☐ other _____

   _____

6. Preliminary list of respondents: _____

   _____

Securing Access to Sites and Respondents

1. a. Permission sought through all appropriate channels (name them) _____

   _____

b. Permission received (from whom? when?)

_____

_____

2. Sites and respondents oriented to evaluation, data collection needs, and schedules (when?)

_____

_____

3. Cooperation of local sites and personnel secured (when? for whom?) _____

_____

4. Confirmatory letter or memo sent? Date?

_____

_____

Instrument Procurement

1. What instruments or schedules need to be developed or selected? Include the due date for each and the person responsible. _____

_____

2. For each one developed:

   ☐ specification completed

   ☐ draft items or questions completed

   ☐ tryout completed

   ☐ revision completed

   ☐ printing and production, if necessary, completed

   ☐ training developed, if needed, and/or directions for administration/completion prepared

3. For each one selected:

   ☐ search completed

   ☐ selection made

   ☐ order placed or duplication arrangements made

   ☐ order received

Data Collection Checklist

1. If additional data collectors are required:

   ☐ data collectors recruited

   ☐ most qualified selected

   ☐ orientation and training, if necessary, conducted

2. Interviews, observations, and other data collection requirements scheduled at each site; written confirmations sent (when? to whom?)

_____

_____

3. If a control group is being used, see Summative Evaluation Guide (Chapter 4) Phase C, Step 2 for relevant checklists.

_____

_____

4. Travel arrangements made, if required

_____

_____

5. Materials and instructions sent out (when?)

_____

_____

6. Emerging issues, new leads, problems documented (what are they?) _____

_____

Data Return Checklist

☐ Data Management System established for tracking returns, coding, organizing, and storing data

☐ ID numbers assigned

☐ Follow-up requests sent out, if necessary

☐ Acceptable return dates achieved

NOTE After data analysis and reporting, the data collection process recycles, possibly requiring the selection of new sites, cases, or respondents to confirm, disconfirm, or extend initial findings, or to respond to emerging issues. If you are using qualitative methods, the data collection process itself will be more iterative, e.g., where one set of interviews and/or observations reveals the need to observe additional settings or seek out the perspectives of additional respondents.

Analyze data with an eye toward program improvement

Instructions

If you are periodically monitoring and examining the program you have probably accumulated a rich and varied set of qualitative and quantitative data. Particularly if there is a control group, you may have collected a battery of measures that can be analyzed using fairly standard statistical methods. How will you synthesize and make sense of what you have? Consider whether you will:

- [ ] Graph results from the various instruments and information sources

- [ ] Perform tests of the statistical significance of differences in performance among groups or from a single group's pretest and posttest

- [ ] Calculate correlations to look for relationships

- [ ] Compute indices of inter-rater reliability

- [ ] Conduct qualitative analyses

How to Measure Performance and Use Tests discusses using test results for statistical analysis on pages 129-151. How to Measure Attitudes describes attitude test scores used for calculating statistics on pages 161-163. See, as well, How to Assess Program Implementation, pages 114-127. Problems of calculating inter-rater reliability are discussed in all three books. Specific statistical analyses are discussed in How to Analyze Data. How to Use Qualitative Methods in Evaluation, Chapter 6, details procedures for analyzing and summarizing qualitative data.

All of the kit's How to books contain suggestions for building graphs and tables to summarize results. For each instrument you use, see the relevant How to book. Consult, as well, Chapter 3 of How to Communicate Evaluation Findings.

Remember that in addition to describing program implementation and the progress in development of skills and attitudes of various participants, you may also need to note whether the program is keeping pace with the time schedule that has been mapped out.

If you have focused data collection on specific program units or components, or if you are conducting pilot tests, then in addition to performing statistical or other analyses, consider whether the program has achieved each of the objectives in question. In particular, examine these things:

- Participant achievement/performance

- Participants' attitudes about the program component in question

- The component's implementation

Consider what kinds of changes could be made that would produce positive results in each of these areas. Below you will find sample cases describing results you might obtain, with suggestions about what to do about each. Determinations of good, poor, and adequate performance should be based on the performance standards set in Step 3.

Sample Case 1

- Achievement/Performance results: Poor
- Attitude results: Good
- Implementation results: Adequate

Participants are happy with the program and implementation is proceeding smoothly. Unfortunately, the program doesn't appear to be working.

- [ ] First, double-check the quality of the performance instrument and its match to program objectives. Is it likely to be sensitive to changes resulting from the program? If the instrument or your indicator is inappropriate, you will have to gather additional data.

- [ ] Can performance results be analyzed at a more detailed level to reveal the specific areas in which achievement/performance is inadequate—e.g., specific skills or behaviors that are lacking? If yes, consider how the program might be augmented to deal better with these specific problems.

☐ Reconsider the program's theory of action, i.e., the chain of assumptions and events that is supposed to lead from program activities to program outcomes. Is there a missing step that needs to be added? Would some reordering or restructuring help? Is the theory faulty? Perhaps new perspectives need to be brought to bear, perspectives which would suggest a modified program plan.

☐ Consider whether there are adequate provisions in the program related to:

- clarity of expectations
- time required for knowledge, skill or behavior development
- the constellation of skills and attitudes required for success
- incentives/motivation
- opportunities for guided application/practice
- feedback on progress toward objectives
- coherence of organization and sequence

☐ Consider whether program assumptions about participants' prerequisites and entering skills are justified. If not, you may need to augment the program to deal with these prerequisites.

Sample Case 2

- Achievement/Performance results: Mixed
- Attitude results: Mixed
- Implementation results: Adequate

Some participants are happy with the program and achieving well; the progress of others is clearly less than satisfactory. The program apparently has been implemented as planned. What do you do?

☐ Consider with what type of participants the program seems to be successful. How are these individuals different from those with whom the program is unsuccessful? How can the program better diagnose and meet the needs of this latter group—or should they be redirected to an alternate program? Consider suggestions in Sample Case 1 for this group.

☐ Consider whether the results are consistently positive in some sites or with some staff and consistently more negative in other sites. What is different about the successful sites, and how could the less effective sites emulate these characteristics/processes? Are there implications for management, staff selection, or training?

Sample Case 3

- Achievement/Performance results: Good
- Program Implementation results: Poor
- Attitude results: Good

What to do? First ask:

☐ Did the achievement/performance measure and the program component address the same objectives? If not, there's your answer! If so, check the technical quality of implementation findings. See How to Assess Program Implementation.

☐ Are you sure that participants' performance and attitudes have changed, or did they start the program that way?—i.e., had the performance and attitude objectives been achieved prior to participants' experience with the program? If, so, reconsider the appropriateness of the objective(s) and of the performance level expectations.

If you haven't yet found an explanation, then ask:

☐ What happened in the program instead of what was planned? Perhaps this should become an official part of the program.

Sample Case 4

More than two of the indicators show unsatisfactory results. In any of these cases, you should investigate the cause of the problem and revise as necessary.

It is a good idea to include planners and staff in the analysis phase and to get their interpretations and perceptions of underlying problems.

Instructions

The key to an effective formative evaluation is good communication. Information about where the program is or is not working needs to be timely and clearly presented.

Phase D has three steps:

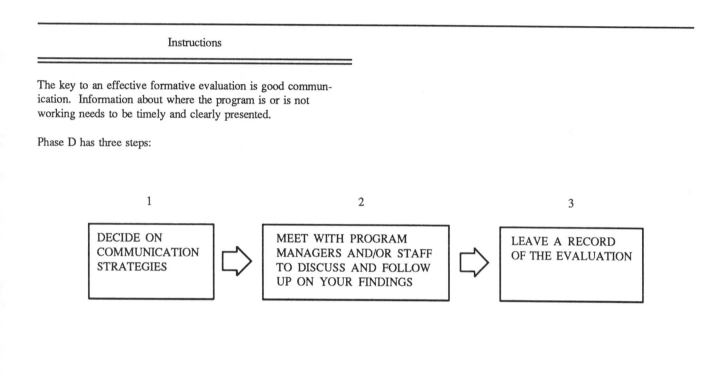

If the manner of reporting and communicating with users was not negotiated during Phase A, decide what strategies you will use and when you will implement them. Remember, because your purpose is to help staff improve the program, the more interactive your communication strategies, the better.

 Consider the full range of strategies available to you:

 informal communication (conversations in the hallway, over coffee, before and and after meetings, etc.)

☐ ad hoc or other presentations at regularly scheduled staff meetings

☐ formal meetings to discuss findings

☐ formal written reports

☐ memos

☐ newsletters

☐ electronic communication

☐ other communication vehicles

 How to Communicate Evaluation Findings, Chapter 2, provides more detail on potential communication options and how to use them.

 Plan on implementing a number of strategies and using them throughout the evaluation period. Provide periodic updates and foster discussion about what you're doing and finding.

 Schedule formal communication activities in advance based both on the program's planning time line and on when findings will be available. Your schedule should reflect two general principles: the more collegial interaction you have with program managers and staff, the more they probably will use your findings; and people can only absorb so much information at a single sitting. In other words, where possible, more frequent, issue-focused meetings are to be preferred over marathon sessions.

Meet with program managers and/or staff to discuss and follow up on your findings

Instructions

You probably will plan periodic meetings with program planners, managers, and/or staff to discuss your findings and their implications for program planning and implementation. Organize your meetings around the specific questions and issues your evaluation was designed to address.

The agenda for your meetings might look something like the following:

Introduction

Review briefly the purposes of the evaluation, the issue(s) or question(s) to be discussed at the meeting, and the source of the data you will be discussing.

Presentation of Results

Display and discuss with your users the data you have collected about each of the target issues or questions. You will want to get the information across quickly, succinctly, and vividly. Therefore, think about the qualitative and quantitative data you have collected and:

 Use graphs or tables summarizing the major quantitative findings you want to report related to each issue. How to Communicate Evaluation Findings, Chapter 3, describes a variety of techniques for displaying data; How to Analyze Data, Chapter 2, also describes in particular how to graph test scores.

 Summarize your qualitative findings related to each issue or question. Use brief anecdotes, typical quotes, etc. to illustrate your findings. How to Use Qualitative Methods in Evaluation, Chapter 6, provides help on how to summarize and interpret such data.

Discussion of the Findings

What do the findings reveal about:

* how the program is operating

* whether it is being implemented as planned

* the strengths and weaknesses of the program

* extra-program factors that are influencing the program

* key problems that have occurred or that might be anticipated

* adequacy of progress toward program outcomes

* the differential effectiveness of the program under particular conditions or with particular individuals? Are the results being influenced by a few extreme cases?

Recommendations

On the basis of the results, what recommendations should be made?

* How, if at all, should the program, its staffing, support, and/or administrative arrangements be modified?

* What are the implications for subsequent evaluation activities?

 Phase C, Step 5, of this manual offers suggestions for interpreting data and deriving recommendations.

 Be prepared to assuage the feelings of potentially defensive staff members, particularly if the results indicate that serious problems exist. Be prepared also to defend the quality of your data.

Leave a record of the evaluation

Instructions

Although the use of your findings for program improvement will depend more on interactive communication strategies, you will still want to leave a lasting though perhaps brief, record of your efforts. Write your report, however, with this admonition in mind: if you've done a good job of communicating to this point, your report will not tell your primary users anything they don't already know.

 Follow the outline and tips given in How to Communicate Evaluation Findings. The report should include briefly:

- A description of why you undertook the evaluation

- Who the primary intended users were

- The kinds of formative questions you intended to ask, the evaluation designs you used, if any, and the methods you used to examine implementation, performance and attitudes

- Less formal data collection methods which you used

- A summary of your findings with each question you addressed

If you have found instruments which were particularly useful, or sensitive to detecting the implementation or effects of the particular program, put them in an appendix.

Your report should conclude with recommendations for future actions or inquiry and suggestions to the summative evaluator, if indeed a summative evaluation of this particular program will be conducted.

 Give the program manager and/or staff an opportunity to review your report in draft form.

This is the end of the Step-by-Step Guides for Conducting a Formative Evaluation. By now evaluation is a familiar topic to you and, we hope, a growing interest. These guides are designed to be used again and again. Perhaps you will want to use them in the future, each time trying a more elaborate design and more sophisticated approach, and adding your own notations of lessons learned and new planning aids.

Chapter 4
Step-by-Step Guides
for Conducting a
Summative Evaluation

The summative evaluator has responsibility for producing an accurate description of the program--complete with measures of its effects--that summarizes both what has transpired during a particular time period and what has been its success. Results from a summative evaluation, usually compiled into a written report, can be used for several purposes:

- To assess for policymakers, funders, managers, or others, the impact of their programs and/or policies
- To document for the funding agency that services promised by the program's planners have indeed been delivered
- To assure that a lasting record of the program remains on file
- To serve as a planning document for people who want to duplicate the program or adapt it to another setting
- To help policymakers and other decisionmakers make decisions about program continuation, expansion, and future funding

The step-by-step guide in this chapter presents the steps to be taken in conducting the summative evaluation of an educational, social service, management, or other program. While the exact procedures to be followed when accomplishing such an evaluation will vary with the setting, summative evaluation in general includes the tasks and follows the sequence described here. The novice to evaluation, for whom this guide is primarily intended, will therefore do well to follow the guide.

This step-by-step guide divides summative evaluation into four *phases,* each corresponding to a major task to be accomplished:

Phase A   Set the Boundaries of the Evaluation
Phase B   Select Appropriate Evaluation Methods
Phase C   Collect and Analyze Information
Phase D   Report Findings

These four phases generally occur in a relatively fixed order, regardless of the content of the evaluation, although what you do during the early phases will often be determined by your plans about how to conduct later ones. Which

tests, measures and other data collection strategies you select during Phase B, for example, will depend on the resources available for data analysis and the information you intend to report later on. This means that many of the decisions guiding the evaluation will need to be made early.

Whenever possible, the step-by-step guide uses checklists and worksheets to help you keep track of what you have decided and found out. Actually, the worksheets might be better called "guidesheets," since you will have to copy many of them onto your own paper rather than use the ones in the book. Space simply does not permit the book to provide places to list large quantities of data.

While the first edition of this *Evaluator's Handbook* focused specifically on evaluating educational programs, this second edition has been designed to meet the needs of a variety of fields. The quest for a more generic approach brings with it some loss in specific guidance and some problems in terminology, particularly in how to designate the various role groups commonly associated with particular programs: those on whom the program is targeted, those who deliver the program, those at various levels who may be responsible for program administration and/or decisionmaking, and other significant constituencies. While no one set of terms perfectly fits all situations, we have chosen to use the following terminology:

Participants—those on whom the project's primary objectives are targeted, e.g., students, clients, patients, employees, residents, at-risk juveniles.

Staff—those primarily responsible for delivering the program to participants, e.g., teachers, clinicians, social workers, probation officers, trainers.

Site managers/administrators—those on-site supervisors responsible for managing overall operations, e.g., principals, supervisors, office managers, chief administrators.

Local or regional managers—those responsible for the operation of a number of local units or sites, e.g., district superintendents, county supervisors, regional directors, and/or administrative staff in intermediate unit settings.

Governing board—those holding fiduciary responsibility for the organization and its operations and/or charged with responsibility for policymaking, e.g., boards of education, boards of trustees.

Community members—significant others in the program environments who are related to the program and its participants, who may both affect and be affected by the program, e.g., parents, local businesses, public at large, other service providers.

Consider now how these terms relate to those in your program situation so that when you see them in the pages which follow, you can substitute the more specific, relevant nomenclature of your field.

As you use the guide, you will come upon references marked by the symbol ◣. These direct you to read sections of various *How to* books contained in the *Program Evaluation Kit*. At these junctures in the evaluation, it will be necessary for you to review a concept or follow a procedure outlined in one of these eight resource books.

- *How to Focus an Evaluation*
- *How to Design a Program Evaluation*
- *How to Use Qualitative Methods in Evaluation*
- *How to Assess Program Implementation*
- *How to Measure Attitudes*
- *How to Measure Performance and Use Tests*
- *How to Analyze Data*
- *How to Communicate Evaluation Findings*

To give you an overview of the summative evaluation tasks included in the guide, a flowchart showing the steps required to complete each phase appears in the introduction to each.

Instructions

Phase A encompasses the evaluation planning period—from the time you accept the job of summative evaluator until you begin to actually carry out the assignments dictated by the role. Much of Phase A amounts to gaining an understanding of the program and outlining the services you can perform, then negotiating them with the agency, staff members, or interested others who will use the information.

The focusing or general planning phase of a summative evaluation is crucial and often difficult. It is a time when you read important documents, talk to people, and think through the whole evaluation. You decide what you do and don't need to know, so that the evaluation you finally carry out is useful to your audiences, accurate in its description of the program, and efficiently carried out.

The five steps of Phase A can be summarized by the following flowchart:

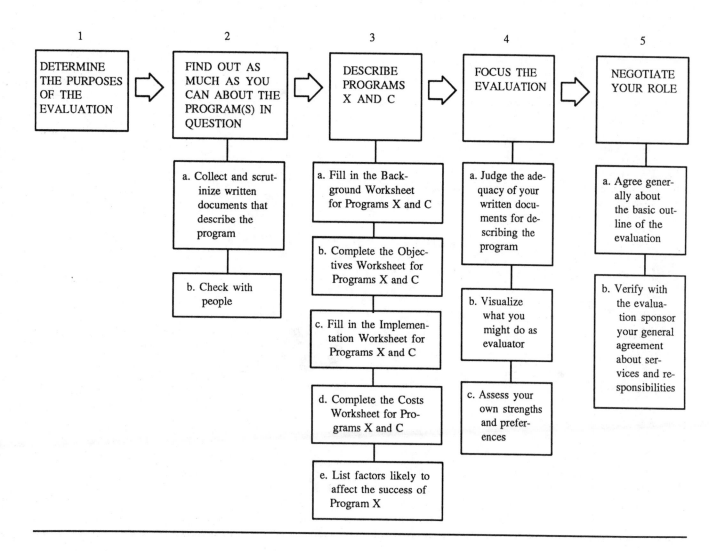

1

DETERMINE THE PURPOSES OF THE EVALUATION

2

FIND OUT AS MUCH AS YOU CAN ABOUT THE PROGRAM(S) IN QUESTION

a. Collect and scrutinize written documents that describe the program

b. Check with people

3

DESCRIBE PROGRAMS X AND C

a. Fill in the Background Worksheet for Programs X and C

b. Complete the Objectives Worksheet for Programs X and C

c. Fill in the Implementation Worksheet for Programs X and C

d. Complete the Costs Worksheet for Programs X and C

e. List factors likely to affect the success of Program X

4

FOCUS THE EVALUATION

a. Judge the adequacy of your written documents for describing the program

b. Visualize what you might do as evaluator

c. Assess your own strengths and preferences

5

NEGOTIATE YOUR ROLE

a. Agree generally about the basic outline of the evaluation

b. Verify with the evaluation sponsor your general agreement about services and responsibilities

Determine the purposes of the evaluation

The job of the summative evaluator is to collect, digest, and report information about a program to satisfy the needs of one or more audiences. The audiences in turn might use the information for any number of purposes:

- To learn about the program

- To satisfy themselves that the program they were promised did indeed occur and, if not, what happened instead

- To make decisions about continuing or discontinuing, expanding or limiting the program, generally through giving or withholding funds

- To clarify an important issue or policy question about the program

If <u>decisions</u> hinge on your findings, your first job is to find out what these decisions are. Likewise, if your evaluation is to clarify particular issues or to answer specific <u>policy questions</u>, you need to determine what they are. Then you will have to ensure that you collect the relevant information and report it to the appropriate audiences.

 Begin your description of the specific purpose of the evaluation and of your primary audience(s) by answering the following questions:

☐ What is the title of the program to be evaluated?

_____

<u>Throughout this chapter, this program will be referred to as Program X.</u>

☐ What decisions will be based on the evaluation?

_____

☐ What primary issues or questions is the evaluation supposed to clarify? _____

_____

☐ Who wants to know about the program? That is, who is the evaluation's primary audience(s)?

- Site Managers/Administrators _____

Report due _____

- Staff _____

Report due _____

- Local or Regional Managers _____

Report due _____

- Governing Board _____

Report due _____

- State Agencies _____

Report due _____

- Federal Agencies _____

Report due _____

- Other Funding Agencies _____

Report due _____

- Community in general _____

Report due _____

- Other (special interest groups, for instance) _____

Report due _____

 Try not to serve too many audiences at once; you can only well serve a limited number of primary users. To produce a credible summative evaluation, your position must allow you to be objective and to focus your attention on a few crucial issues. See pages 31 and 33 of this handbook for elaboration of this critical admonition.

 Ask the people who constitute your primary users this question:

☐ What would be done if Program X were to be found inadequate? _____

_____

_____

Here name another program or the old program, or indicate that they would have no program at all. What you enter in this blank is the alternative with which Program X should be compared. There could be many alternatives or competitors; but select the most likely alternative.

This most likely alternative to Program X, its closest competitor, is referred to throughout this guide as Program C. Write it after the word "or" in the next sentence:

A choice must be made between continuing Program X or . . .

_____

_____

This is Program C.

☐ Has one of the evaluation's audiences, such as a federal or state funding agency, stated specific requirements for this evaluation? Are you required, for instance, to use particular tests, to assess attainment of particular outcomes, or to report on special forms? If so, summarize these evaluation requirements by quoting or referencing the documents that stipulate them.

_____

_____

_____

_____

_____

CALENDAR What is the absolute deadline for the earliest evaluation report? Record the earliest of the dates you listed when describing audiences.

An evaluation report must be ready by

_____

Is there a set budget for the evaluation? What is it?

_____

The budget available for the evaluation project is:

_____

Find out as much as you can about the program(s) in question

a. Collect and scrutinize written documents that describe the program. If you are planning a comparative study, examine the documents for Program C as well.

CHECK ✓

☐ A program proposal written for the funding agency

☐ The request for proposals (RFP) written by the sponsor or funding agency to which this program's proposal was a response

☐ Results of a needs assessment whose findings the program is intended to address

☐ Written federal, state, regional, district, or other guidelines about program processes and goals to which this program must conform

☐ The program's budget, particularly the part that mentions the evaluation

☐ A description of, or an organizational chart depicting, the administrative and staff roles played by various people in the program

☐ Guides for the activities or materials which have been purchased for the program

☐ Past evaluations of this or similar programs

☐ Lists of goals and objectives which the staff or planners feel describe the program's aims

☐ Tests, surveys, or other assessments which the program planners feel could be used to measure the effects of the program

☐ Assessments that were used by the program's formative evaluator, if there was one

☐ Memos, meeting minutes, newspaper articles, brochures—descriptions made by the staff or the planners of the program

☐ Descriptions of the program's history or of the social context into which it has been designed to fit

☐ Articles in the professional and evaluation literature that describe the effects of programs such as the one in question, its materials, or its various subcomponents

☐ Other _____

Once you have discovered which materials are available, seek them out and copy them if possible.

Take notes in the margins. Write down, or dictate onto tape, comments about your general impression of the program, its context, and staff. This will get you started on writing your own description of the program. You may want to complete Step 3 concurrently with this general overview. Be alert, in particular, for the following details:

☐ The program's major general goals. List separately those that seem to be of highest priority to planners, the community, or the program's sponsors. Note where these priorities differ across audiences since your report to each should reflect the priorities of each.

_____

☐ Specifically stated objectives

_____

☐ The philosophy or point of view of the program planners—and sponsors, if these differ

_____

☐ Examples of similar programs that planners intend to emulate

_____

☐ Writers in the field whose point of view the program is intended to mirror

_____

☐ The needs of the community or constituency which the program is intended to meet—whether these have been explicitly stated or seem to implicitly underlie the program

☐ Program implementation directives and requirements, described in the proposal, required by the sponsor, or both

☐ The amount of variation expected in the program from site to site, or even from participant to participant

☐ The number and distribution of sites involved

☐ Plans which have been developed describing how the program looks in operation—schedules, activities or component plans, etc.

☐ Administrative, decision-making, and staff/teaching roles played by various people

☐ Management responsibilities

☐ Participant evaluation plans

☐ Staff evaluation plans

☐ Program evaluation plans

☐ Descriptions of program aspirations that have been stated as percentages of participants achieving certain objectives and/or deadlines by which particular objectives should be reached.

b. Check with people.

Check your description of the program against the impressions and aspirations of your primary audiences and of the program's planners and staff. By all means, contact the people who will be in the best position to use the information you collect, your primary users. Verify again how they plan to use the information.

Try to think at this time of other people whose actions, opinions, and decisions will influence the success of the evaluation and the extent to which the information you collect will be useful and used. Try to talk with each of these people, either at a group meeting or individually. Seek out in particular:

☐ Administrative personnel not directly connected with the project, but whose cooperation will help you carry out the evaluation more efficiently or quickly. Negotiate access to the program!

☐ Influential community members or board members whose support will help the evaluation go more smoothly

☐ Evaluators who have worked with this particular program or programs like it. They will have valuable advice to give about what information to collect, how, and from whom.

If key people are too busy to talk, send them memos. Describe the evaluation, what you would like them to do for you, and when.

If possible, observe the program in operation or programs like it. Take a field trip in the company of program planners and staff. Have them point out the program's key components and major variations.

Take careful notes of everything you see and hear. Later you may find some of these valuable.

Describe Programs X and C

Instructions

In this step, outline the distinctive features of Program X and that received by the competitor or control group you have chosen to use, Program C. Of course, if there will be no competitor, you will not have to fill in the boxes that refer to it.

Writing this section will also help you rough out the introductory sections of the eventual evaluation report.

How to Communicate Evaluation Findings, Chapter 4, contains an outline of what you should include in your description of the goals and primary characteristics of the program. How to Assess Program Implementation, Appendix, lists in detail the questions you might answer in your description of how the program looks.

If both Program X and Program C are likely contenders for adoption, then both are the foci of the evaluation. Both should be described in the greatest detail possible. If Program C is no program or one that is not an alternative to X, then describe what happens to the control group generally, with a focus on the chances its members might have to pick up what Program X intends to accomplish.

Worksheets like the following will help you organize your descriptions of the programs.

a. Fill in the worksheet for comparing the backgrounds of Programs X and C.

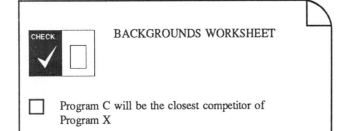

CHECK ✓

BACKGROUNDS WORKSHEET

☐ Program C will be the closest competitor of Program X

☐ Program C will be a control group receiving either no program or one that is not a contender

☐ There will be no competitor or control group

- Title of Program X _____

  Title of Program C _____

- Sites of Program X _____

  Sites of Program C _____

People Affected by Programs X and C

Staff

- Who are the staff for Program X?
  _____
  _____

  Who are the staff for Program C?
  _____
  _____

- What characteristics are required of staff employed in Program X, e.g., professional background, language abilities, subject area skills, teaching experience, in-service training? _____
  _____

  In Program C?
  _____
  _____

- Administrators/Managers involved in Program X?
  _____
  _____

  In Program C?
  _____
  _____

- Other staff for Program X?

_____

_____

For Program C?

_____

_____

- Consultants or other specialists for Program X?

_____

_____

For Program C?

_____

_____

Parents or Community Members

- Are special permissions needed for individuals to participate in Program X? _____

  In Program C? _____

- Were parents or community members to be actively involved in the program activities in X? ☐   C? ☐

  Were they to have an advisory role in X? ☐   C? ☐

Program Origins

- How did Program X get started?

_____

_____

Was there a needs assessment? _____

- How did Program C get started?

_____

_____

Was there a needs assessment? _____

- Official demands on the programs

  What legal or funding demands or restrictions have been placed on Program X?

_____

_____

On Program C?

_____

_____

NOTE Note where background characteristics of the programs—for instance, relative experience of staff—might reduce the comparability of Programs X and C.

_____

_____

b. Complete the worksheet for comparing the goals and objectives of Programs X and C to help you clarify what you expect to be the results or outcomes of the two programs.

List the desired outcomes of Program X on the worksheet below. Try to make at least one entry in each blank; this will help you think of outcomes that you might not have otherwise considered. Leave blanks empty only where you think listing outcomes would be totally irrelevant.

NOTE Keep careful track of how closely the competitor or control group's desired outcomes correspond with those of Program X. If Program C is a competitor to Program X rather than a control group, then the two programs probably strive for quite a few of the same outcomes. If Program C is a no-program control group, then possibly none of its desired outcomes coincide with Program X. This is OK for now. It should be taken into account, however, when you interpret your results.

OBJECTIVES WORKSHEET

Desired Performance Outcomes of Program X: Cognitive and Psychomotor

- At the end of Program X, the participants will have achieved or changed as follows

_____

_____

- At the end of Program X, the staff will have achieved or changed as follows _____

_____

- At the end of Program X, community members will have achieved or changed as follows

_____

- At the end of Program X, others will have achieved or changed as follows _____

Desired Performance Outcomes of Program C: Cognitive and Psychomotor

• At the end of Program C, the participants will have achieved or changed as follows _____

_____

• At the end of Program C, the staff will have achieved or changed as follows _____

_____

• At the end of Program C, community members will have achieved or changed as follows

_____

• At the end of Program C, others will have achieved or changed as follows _____

_____

Desired Outcomes of Program X: Affective/Attitudinal

• At the end of Program X, the participants will have the following attitude(s)

_____

• At the end of Program X, the staff will have the following attitude(s) _____

_____

• At the end of Program X, community members will have the following attitude(s)

_____

• At the end of Program X, others will have the following attitude(s) _____

_____

Desired Outcomes of Program C: Affective/Attitudinal

• At the end of Program C, the participants will have the following attitude(s)

_____

• At the end of Program C, the staff will have the following attitude(s) _____

_____

• At the end of Program C, community members will have the following attitude(s)

_____

_____

• At the end of Program C, others will have the following attitude(s) _____

_____

Other Desired Outcomes of Program X: political, organizational, social, etc. _____

_____

_____

Other Desired Outcomes of Program C: political, organizational, social, etc. _____

_____

_____

Now, go back and make sure that outcomes most valued by your primary intended users—particularly the funding agency—appear on the lists of outcomes you just completed.

Do you need to meet with or poll your users to find out more exactly what they want to know, what they already know, and what their goals are for the program? If so, now is the time to do so. Use the outcomes listed in the step to structure your meeting. Amend it according to the decisions made there. Add and subtract outcomes if necessary.

Once you are sure that all the desired outcomes are listed on the outcomes chart, go back over it and rank the outcomes you have listed in order of importance—#1 will be the most crucial outcome that the program is supposed to achieve, #2 the next more important, and so forth. This ranking will serve as a guide to planning what to measure in Phase B.

C. Fill in the Implementation Worksheet. It describes the materials, arrangements, and activities that constitute Programs X and C.

The purpose of this worksheet is to help you define the activities, services, and organizational arrangements that are crucial to the implementation of the programs you are comparing. Once these activities are defined, you can give some thought to how you will assess their execution. Although different programs place various amounts of emphasis on precise execution of particular activities, virtually all of them specify some activities that are to take place. In fact, some—such as open classrooms or quality circles—might focus more closely on appropriate enactment of program processes and activities than upon immediate achievement of outcomes.

In any case, list the most crucial activities, services, and arrangements of Programs X and C in the table below. Of course, if there will be no competitor or control group, then write no program over the Program C questions.

```
┌─────────────────────────────────────────────────┐
│                                              ╲   │
│          IMPLEMENTATION WORKSHEET             ╲  │
│                                               │  │
│  Resources                                       │
│                                                  │
│  • New activities, services, materials, or       │
│    sequences introduced for Program X _____     │
│    _____          │
│    _____          │
│                                                  │
│    For Program C _____     │
│    _____          │
│    _____          │
│                                                  │
│  • Nature of staff configurations and/or of      │
│    staff/participant interactions for Program X  │
│    _____          │
│                                                  │
│    For Program C _____     │
│    _____          │
│                                                  │
│  • Equipment—projectors, laboratory equipment,   │
│    etc.—purchased for Program X _____     │
│    _____          │
│                                                  │
│    For Program C _____     │
│    _____          │
│                                                  │
│  • Facilities—number of classrooms, special      │
│    spaces, etc.—allotted for Program X _____    │
│    _____          │
│                                                  │
│    For Program C _____     │
│    _____          │
│                                                  │
│  • Time allocations in Program X _____     │
│    _____          │
│                                                  │
│    For Program C _____     │
│    _____          │
│                                                  │
│  • Other—Program X _____     │
│    _____          │
│                                                  │
│    Other—Program C _____     │
│    _____          │
│                                                  │
└─────────────────────────────────────────────────┘
```

Activities

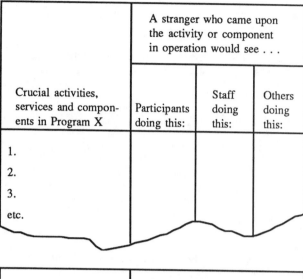

Crucial activities, services and components in Program X	A stranger who came upon the activity or component in operation would see . . .		
	Participants doing this:	Staff doing this:	Others doing this:
1.			
2.			
3.			
etc.			

Crucial activities, services and components in Program C	A stranger who came upon the activity or component in operation would see . . .		
	Participants doing this:	Staff doing this:	Others doing this:
1.			
2.			
3.			
etc.			

Consult, as well, Chapter 2 of How to Assess Program Implementation. It lists questions to ask the staff and planners of both programs to help them describe implementation in detail.

If it falls within your job role to critique the programs as well as describe them and their relative effectiveness, then at this point make a judgment about the clarity and coherence of each program's goals and rationale. Ask yourself:

• Are the goals and objectives stated precisely enough to be understood by the program's staff and constituency?

• Or are they so unclear that they detract from the program's sense of common purpose?

• Is the rationale underpinning both programs logical and well thought out?

• Or is there confusion or misunderstanding about why the program's activities should lead to its intended outcomes?

d. Complete the worksheet for comparing the costs of Programs X and C.

The purpose of this worksheet is to help you clarify informally the costs you want to check in order to evaluate Programs X and C. These costs could be qualitative, such as drains on staff energy, and dollar costs such as the cost of materials. Both Program X and Program C will have associated costs.

 List below three or four possible major costs brought about by each program.

COSTS WORKSHEET	
Expected Costs— Qualitative	Expected Costs— Dollars
List here qualitative non-money costs that might occur such as extra fatigue. Do not forget opportunity costs of each program—that is, things foregone in order to implement the program. Be careful to also list possible negative effects of each program on those not in the program, such as resentment, less access to professional help, etc.	List here those facets of each program that will require spending extra dollars--dollars that might have been spent as a matter of course if the program were not implemented. Estimate these costs when costs can be more exactly determined.
The following negative consequences might occur as a result of Program X _____ _____	The following amount of money will be spent over and above what is usually spent as a result of Program X _____ _____
The following negative consequences might occur as a result of Program C _____ _____	The following amount of money will be spent over and above what is usually spent as a result of Program C _____ _____

 Be careful when delineating costs to differentiate start-up costs from continuation costs. Start-up costs occur at the beginning of the program. Some quantitative start-up costs might result from purchasing equipment, materials, training, etc. A qualitative start-up cost might be poor morale due to initial disorganization. Start-up costs, unless they are massive and unlikely to diminish the next time the program occurs, will likely be of less interest in a summative evaluation than continuation costs. These latter are incurred by day-to-day program operation—for instance, salaries, chronic materials replacement, or opportunity costs such as poor morale.

 Look over the costs and benefits worksheet, and check the one-time-only costs.

 How to Communicate Evaluation Findings, pages 104-106, lists some additional questions to consider when preparing to measure costs.

e. List factors likely to affect the success of Program X. Is it likely to be equally successful in all sites, or are there contextual influences that will mediate its effectiveness (e.g., leadership support, staff ownership, staff training, staff preferences, participant background characteristics)?

_____

_____

_____

---

a. Judge the adequacy of your written documents and other available data for describing the program.

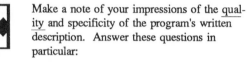 Make a note of your impressions of the quality and specificity of the program's written description. Answer these questions in particular:

- Are the written documents and the information you have otherwise gathered specific enough to give you a good picture of the key elements of the program and its intended outcomes? Do they suggest what components you will evaluate and what they will look like?

  ☐ yes   ☐ no   ☐ uncertain

  _____
  _____

- Do the important program constituencies/your primary audiences agree on what the program is supposed to be accomplishing and on the key processes, arrangements, and activities that constitute the program?

  ☐ yes   ☐ no   ☐ uncertain

  _____
  _____

If your answer to any of these questions is no or uncertain, then you will have to include in your evaluation plans further discussions with constituency groups and the sponsors to articulate program goals and key processes; you may also want to consider a qualitative approach, or limit the audiences for your report.

b. Visualize what you might do as evaluator.

 Base this exercise upon your impressions of the program:

- Is the program sufficiently mature to warrant a summative evaluation? If no, consider persuading your sponsor that a formative evaluation approach is more appropriate.

- What comparison or control groups can be used?

 Consult Chapter 1 of How to Design a Program Evaluation for ideas about using control group designs. Chapter 1 describes evaluation designs, some of them fairly unorthodox, which might be useful for situations where control groups are difficult to set up. Using a control group greatly increases the interpretability of your information by providing a basis of comparison from which to judge the results that you obtain. Pages 26 to 35 of the same book describe different sets of control groups and the programs they might receive.

- Which components appear to provide the key to whether the program sinks or swims? _____

  _____

- Which components do the planners and staff most emphasize as critically important? _____

  _____

- Which outcomes are of highest priority? _____

  _____

- Which outcomes will probably be easiest to accomplish? Which will be most difficult? _____

  _____

- What effects might the program have that its planners have not anticipated? _____

  _____

- What information about program context, participant or staff characteristics, etc., do you need to answer policy questions of interest? _____

  _____

- What outcomes, program processes, and characteristics will require quantitative data? Where will qualitative data be helpful? _____

  _____

• What permissions/clearances are needed for various
  evaluation activities? _____
  _____
  _____

• How much participant, administrator, etc. time will be
  available for evaluation activities? _____
  _____
  _____

• What records or other data are already available?
  _____
  _____

When you think about the service you can provide, you will,
of course, need to consider three important things besides
program characteristics and outcomes. These are the budget
which you uncovered in Step 1, time constraints, and your
own particular strengths and talents.

C. Assess your own strengths and preferences.

You will best benefit the program in those
areas where your visualization in Step 4b
matches your expertise. You should "tune"
the evaluation to build on your skills as:

☐   An experimental researcher

☐   A qualitative methodologist

☐   A measurement expert

☐   A subject area or program expert

☐   A facilitator for problem solving

☐   A good interviewer or observer

☐   Other _____

Consult, as well, How to Focus an Evaluation. It lists additional questions and
concerns you will want to consider.

Instructions

Chapter 2 presented a general outline of the tasks that often fall within the summative evaluator's role. You will have to work out your own job with your own sponsor and primary users. Meet again and confer with the people whose cooperation will be necessary—those whose decisions about the program carry most influence and who will cooperate when you gather information. You may, of course, also want to meet with other audiences.

 During this step you want to obtain your sponsor's agreement on the general outline of your evaluation plan. The details of this general outline will be filled in during Phase B.

a. Agree generally about the basic outline of the evaluation.

☐ Agree generally about the program characteristics and outcomes that will be your major focus—regardless of the prominence given them in official program descriptions.

 Which outcomes? Look at the Objectives Worksheet in Step 3b, beginning on page 95. It lists the desired outcomes of Programs X and C in order of priority. For now, simply circle the most important ones that are common to both programs—the ones you know you will need to discuss plus others that are of great interest to your sponsor.

 Which activities? While it is important to know how the programs looked, what you describe about each program in your report—as well as which aspects of your description you decide to support with backup data—will vary according to your role and the situation.

 Chapter 1 of How to Assess Program Implementation asks questions to help you decide which of the features listed in the

Implementation Worksheet, page 97, you should document. Confer with sponsors and other interested audiences to help with your decision making.

 Which costs? Dollar costs listed on the Costs Worksheet, page 98, will not be hard to measure; you can consult your records for this. Plan to measure all the dollar costs of Programs X and C, if it is a competitor. Qualitative costs will be more difficult both to define and to measure but circle two that you plan to measure per program. Number them 1 and 2 in order of priority.

 Consult Chapter 1 of this handbook, pages 22 to 24, for additional discussion on the topic of what to measure.

 Which other factors? You listed other factors that will influence program success in Step 3e, page 98. Select those which have the greatest policy implications, e.g., in making decisions about where to expand the program, in formulating selection criteria for the program, and in deciding where and how the program needs strengthening.

It is critical that you allocate sufficient resources to finding out what the sponsor and other key audiences most want to know. Confer with them to validate your initial decisions; ask them:

• Which outcomes, achievements, and attitudes are of highest priority? _____

• On which outcomes, achievements, and attitudes do you expect the program to have the most direct and easily observed effect? _____

• Does the program have social or political objectives that should be assessed? _____

• Which characteristics of the program do you consider most important for accomplishing its objectives? _____

☐ Agree about other contextual factors that need to be investigated _____

☐ Agree generally about the sites and people from whom you will collect information. Ask these questions:

• At which sites is the program in operation? How geographically dispersed are they? _____

• How much does the program vary from site to site? Where do such variations occur? _____

• Who are the important people to talk with and observe? _____

• When are the most critical times to see the program--occasions over its duration, and also hours during the day? _____

• At what points during the course of the program will it be best to assess participant outcomes, staff attitudes, etc? Are there logical points at, say, the completion of a course or subsequently?

 More detailed description of sampling plans is contained in How to Assess Program Implementation, Chapter 3. How to Design a Program Evaluation, pages 35 to 48, describes decisions you might make about when to make measurements.

☐ Agree about the part the staff will play in collecting and providing information.

• Can record-keeping systems be established to give me needed information? _____

• Will staff be able to share achievement/performance information with me or help with its collection? Are they willing to administer tests to samples of students? _____

 How to Assess Program Implementation, Chapter 4, describes ways to use records kept during the program to back up descriptions of its implementation.

☐ Agree about the extent to which you will be able to implement an experimental approach in the evaluation. Find out:

• Will it be possible to set up control groups with whom program outcomes can be compared? _____

• Will it be possible to establish a true control group design by randomly assigning participants to different variations of the program or to a no-program control group? Will it be possible to delay introducing the program at some sites? _____

• Can non-equivalent control groups be formed or located? _____

• Will I have a chance to make measurements prior to the program and/or often enough to set up a time series design? _____

• Will I be able or required to conduct in-depth case studies at some sites? _____

 Details about the use of designs in evaluation are discussed in How to Design a Program Evaluation. See in particular pages 48 to 54 and 56 to 62. Case studies are discussed in How to Assess Program Implementation, pages 30 to 33 and in How to Use Qualitative Methods in Evaluation.

b. Verify with the evaluation sponsor your general agreement about services and responsibilities.

Before launching into an intensive and detailed evaluation planning process, you will want to agree about the general outline of services you intend to provide and the minimum budget that will be available to you. You will enter into a more detailed contract agreement at the end of Phase B.

 You may want to document this agreement in the form of a memo to the sponsor.

Your agreement should cover:

☐ The purpose of the evaluation _____

☐ The general approach you plan to use (<u>what</u> you will assess and <u>how</u>):

- The kinds of program outcomes you will examine

  _____

  _____

- The types of program characteristics/processes you will examine

  _____

  _____

- Participant and staff characteristics

  _____

  _____

- Other context data

  _____

  _____

- Data collection approaches

  _____

  _____

☐ Design and analysis plans and the questions they will address

☐ When and to whom you will provide reports

☐ Any assumptions you have about staff and other resources that will be available to you from the program (e.g., program records, staff time to administer instruments, random assignment options)

☐ Budget available

 Don't become too detailed at this point, as you will want to give yourself as much flexibility as possible for Phase B plans. Consider this agreement as a statement of the <u>minimum</u> you will be providing, stated at a level of generality that retains some options. For example, while you will want to agree on important outcomes and program processes you will examine and on the type of data collection approaches that you will generally employ, you should not at this point necessarily commit to specific instruments.

Select Appropriate Evaluation Methods

Instructions

In Phase A, Set the Boundaries of the Evaluation, you made a number of decisions determining the form of the evaluation you are conducting:

- You acquainted yourself with the uses to which the information you collect will be put.

- You decided whether the evaluation will involve a competitor or a control group.

- You made tentative lists of and reached tentative agreements on the outcomes, activities, and costs that you might measure to gauge the success of the program of interest relative to the control program, if any, and of other information you might need to answer policy questions of interest.

In Phase B, you will:

- Select data collection approaches and instruments.

- Choose an evaluation design, based partly on your access to control groups, for each measure or data collection technique you plan. Probably just one or two designs will underlie the whole evaluation.

- Estimate how much your evaluation will cost—and trim accordingly.

- Come to a final agreement on the evaluation services you will provide.

Phase B's eight steps and their substeps can occur simultaneously. A common sequence, however, is described in this flowchart:

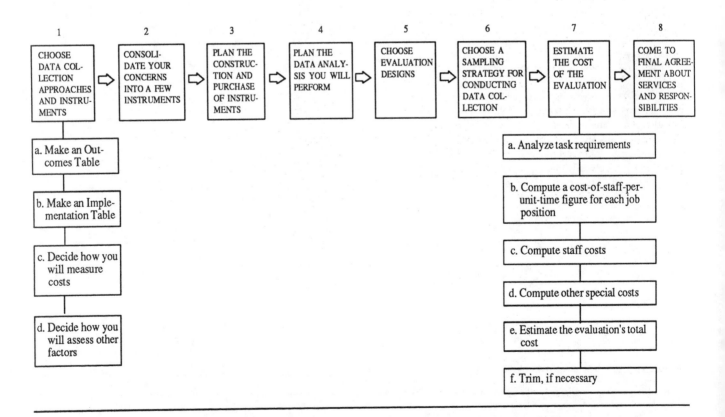

Choose data collection approaches and instruments

Instructions

The purpose of this step is the selection and planning of data collection approaches and instruments—tests, questionnaires, diaries, observations, etc.—that will give you the best possible set of information.

a. Make an Outcomes Table with five vertical numbered columns.

 In Column 1 list the outcomes common to both Programs X and C that you have chosen to assess. These are the circled objectives on the Objectives Worksheet, pages 95 and 96, those you have agreed to examine in Phase A, Step 5, plus additions that you want to examine as a result of discussions with sponsors or based on your own hunches. If you intend to measure outcomes unique to one of the programs, list these as well, but remember that Programs X and C are not competitors regarding these.

Outcomes Table

1 Outcomes	2 Circle C, A, P, or O*	3 Method chosen	4 Source of data/to be given to whom?	5 Existing instrument or needs to be developed'
1. 2 etc. Those unique to X: 1. 2. etc. Those unique to C: 1. 2. etc.	C A P O C A P O C A P O C A P O C A P O C A P O			

*Cognitive, Affective, Psychomotor, Other

 For advice about measuring cognitive or psychomotor objectives, see How to Measure Performance and Use Tests. If objectives are affective, see How to Measure Attitudes. If selected methods are qualitative, see How to Use Qualitative Methods in Evaluation.

 For each objective, list the assessment method chosen in Column 3—i.e., tests, questionnaires, interviews, observations, records; the recipients of the method in Column 4; and in Column 5 whether a specific instrument already exists to implement the method or one needs to be developed.

b. Make a four-column Implementation Table.

List in Column 1 the materials, activities, services, and organizational arrangements in Program X and Program C which you will investigate.

Implementation Table

1 Activities, services, organizational arrangements, materials	2 Method chosen	3 Source of data/to be administered to whom?	4 Existing instrument or needs to be developed
Of Program X 1. 2. 3. 4. etc. Of Program C 1. 2. etc.			

Consult How to Assess Program Implementation and How to Use Qualitative Methods in Evaluation for suggestions about ways to collect data to support your description of program activities.

Then enter in Column 2 the methods you have chosen to use. In Column 3, list recipients of the methods—i.e., the source of your data. Finally, in Column 4, indicate whether an instrument already exists for the selected method or whether one needs to be developed.

NOTE Plan to collect data from a variety of sources of information and to solicit the perspectives of a variety of groups. Thus, for each outcome, implementation, cost, and other factors you include, you may want to list more than one method and/or more than one respondent group.

c. Decide how you will measure costs.

Choose which instruments will give you the information you need, and enter these instruments into a three-column Costs Table.

Costs Table

1 Costs	2 Method chosen	3 Source of data/ to be given to whom?
1. 2. 3. etc.		

d. Decide how you will assess other factors.

Choose which instruments will give you the information you need, and enter these instruments into a three-column Other Factors Table.

Other Factors Table

1 Other Factors	2 Method chosen	3 Source of data/ to be given to whom?
1. 2. 3. etc.		

Instructions

If you want to collect a maximum amount of information per instrument, try the following quick exercise in re-listing. If you are satisfied that your list of instruments is efficient, or if it is very small, skip this step.

In the interest of economy of time and money, and so that your evaluation is not intrusive on the program, try to administer only one instrument of a particular type—questionnaire, interview, test, etc.—to each group of respondents. For example, do not give teachers a questionnaire on costs and a questionnaire on attitudes. Consolidate concerns about outcomes, implementation, and costs into single instruments.

 If your evaluation focuses on many concerns and several types of instruments will be administered, then try filling in this three-column table to help you organize your thoughts:

1 Method chosen	2 Source of data/ to be given to whom?	3 Outcome, activity, or cost (and its number from Step 2)
1. 2. 3. 4. etc.		

 To complete the table, go back and look at the outcomes, aspects of program implementation, costs, and other factors you listed on the tables you completed in Step 1 of this phase.

Then:

• List in Column 1 each instrument you have chosen to administer.

• In Column 2, note the group to whom it will be given (participants, staff, district administrators, School Board, etc.).

• In the third column, list the evaluation concerns—outcomes, implementation characteristics, costs, and their numbers—that the instrument will cover.

When an instrument and a to whom listed in Columns 1 and 2 match a pair that has already been listed, enter only the corresponding concern in Column 3. This will allow you to collect concerns per instrument, producing lists like this:

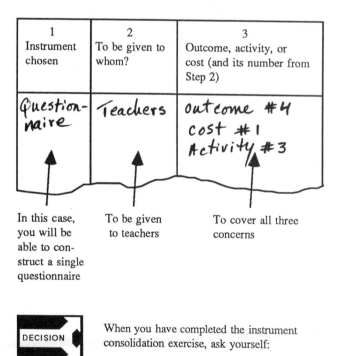

1 Instrument chosen	2 To be given to whom?	3 Outcome, activity, or cost (and its number from Step 2)
Question-naire	Teachers	outcome #4 cost #1 Activity #3

In this case, you will be able to construct a single questionnaire

To be given to teachers

To cover all three concerns

DECISION When you have completed the instrument consolidation exercise, ask yourself:

☐ Can I collect yet more information? _____

Look for instruments that will cover <u>only</u> one evaluation
concern—for example:

Then ask yourself:

☐   Could I add to the value of using the instrument by
    measuring a concern listed in Phase A that I did not
    bring forward to the tables in Phase B, Step 2?

 Go back over the worksheets you completed
when you listed major features of the program during Phase A. With a little extra
effort, you might add a new concern that can
be easily assessed. For example, if you have chosen to use
"observation" to measure the implementation of a behavior
modification system in the classroom, it may be possible to
add <u>another activity</u> that your observer could keep track of—
say, topics of instruction in math, or length of time spent on
reading—to the list of concerns. This will allow you to take
maximum advantage of data collection opportunities. Be-
ware, however, that you don't unconsciously sacrifice depth
or try to accomplish too much.

If you can think of <u>no</u> outcomes, activities, or costs to be
added to instruments now measuring only one, then consider
one final question:

☐   Is that <u>one</u> single concern worth the effort of devoting
    one whole instrument—with all the time and effort
    involved in construction, administration, and scoring—
    to it?

If the concern is of high priority and you—or your audience—<u>must</u> know about it, then the answer is YES. Use the
instrument. If the answer is NO, then consider eliminating
the instrument and try to measure that concern in some other
way.

Plan the construction and purchase of instruments

Instructions

Once you have a list of the instruments you will administer, use this step to help you to manage their acquisition and to plan their use.

 If you suspect that you have listed more instruments than you can realistically develop or purchase and administer within the time and cost limits of your evaluation, then do this: complete Step 8 in this phase to get a more realistic perspective on how much the evaluation will cost. If you still think your data collection plans are too ambitious, select a few instruments that measure the outcomes, activities, or costs that you feel are most important, and obtain these instruments first. If time and funds are available, you can acquire the others later.

 Find out, as well, whether members of the program's staff are willing to help with collecting data. Explain to program directors and staff members that their cooperation will allow you to collect richer and more credible information about the program—to present, in the end, a clearer and more fair picture of what has been accomplished.

Ask them in particular:

☐ Can records kept during the program as a matter of course be collected or copied to provide information for the evaluation? _____

☐ Can record-keeping systems be established and maintained to give the needed evaluation information? _____

☐ Will staff be able to share outcome information with the evaluator or help with its collection? Are you willing to administer instruments to samples of participants or others? _____

☐ Will one or more staff members be willing to assist with collecting information, constructing or scoring instruments, or overseeing proper implementation of the evaluation design? _____

 How to Assess Program Implementation, pages 63 to 71, describes a method for establishing a record-keeping system to keep track of program activities during its evaluation.

 Now is the time to delegate responsibilities. You may be able to relieve yourself of some of the burden of conducting this evaluation by finding staff members or volunteers from local schools and colleges. These people can order and construct instruments, see to their administration, and set up the evaluation design described in Step 5 of Phase B and Step 2 of Phase C.

 Lend your assistants copies of a How to book that describes construction or purchase of the instruments you need. Or give them How to Design a Program Evaluation. Agree together on deadlines for construction or acquisition as well as administration of instruments. Step 1 of Phase C will help you set realistic deadlines.

 Build a schedule. Use a table like the one on the following page to record your decisions about construction, purchase, and delegation of responsibilities regarding instruments. The relevant How to books give form letters and memos for ordering tests from publishers.

Instrument Management Table

1	2	3	4	5
Instrument chosen	Made in-house or purchased?	Person responsible for construction/acquisition	Date instrument to be received or completed	Steps required

 Various books in the Program Evaluation Kit contain advice on constructing instruments. The relevant How to books guide you in construction or revision of:

Checklists	How to Assess Program Implementation and How to Measure Attitudes
Interviews	How to Measure Attitudes, How to Assess Program Implementation, and How to Use Qualitative Methods in Evaluation
Achievement tests	How to Measure Performance and Use Tests
Observation schedule	How to Assess Program Implementation, How to Measure Attitudes, and How to Use Qualitative Methods in Evaluation
Questionnaires for different age groups	How to Measure Attitudes and How to Assess Program Implementation
Records	How to Assess Program Implementation
Attitude rating scales	How to Measure Attitudes
Sociometric instruments	How to Measure Attitudes

Plan the data analysis you will perform with the results from each instrument

---

Instructions

As soon as you have decided what instruments you will use and have roughed out the contents of each, plan how you will analyze the data that each will produce. Organize your plans according to each of the major evaluation questions or issues your study is to address. Considering data analysis early in the evaluation will help to ensure you collect the right information and will prevent you from wasting time collecting information you will not use—or worse yet, collecting the right information, but in a form too unwieldy to be used.

 Each of the How to books in the Program Evaluation Kit makes suggestions for summarizing, analyzing, and displaying data.

	See pages
How to Measure Attitudes	159-177
How to Measure Performance and Use Tests	122-151
How to Assess Program Implementation	114-127
How to Use Qualitative Methods in Evaluation	144-170

How to Design a Program Evaluation contains tables, graphs, and analyses associated with each of the evaluation designs you might choose. Try to collect information in the form that can be most easily presented and discussed.

How to Analyze Data describes some of the more straight-forward analyses you might perform. If you want more complex statistics, consult a data analyst. Carefully examine the match between the analyses you plan to use and the measures you are planning before you become too deeply enmeshed in constructing instruments.

 If at all possible, plan now whether your analyses will be by hand or computer. These are discussed in the kit's measurement books. For a more detailed description of computer data analysis, see How to Analyze Data.

Choose evaluation designs

Instructions

An evaluation design is a plan of who will receive each assessment instrument you decide to administer—or who will be the subjects of a qualitative data collection—and when. The quality of the design directly affects the validity and usefulness of your empirical results.

 Read pages 20 to 21 of this handbook. These present an argument for using designs in evaluation. If you have not read How to Design a Program Evaluation, look at Chapters 1 and 2 now. This book discusses in detail six designs for quantitative approaches and gives directions for implementing each one. Pages 44 to 69 in How to Use Qualitative Methods in Evaluation discuss design issues in qualitative approaches.

 Choose a design to guide administration of each instrument. Read How to Design a Program Evaluation, pages 48 to 54, and the following discussion about designs. Then decide which ones you can implement.

Because it is usually inconvenient—and unnecessary—to use a separate design per instrument, choose one or two to underpin the whole evaluation. Designs 1, 2, 3, and 5 are the most useful for gathering interpretable information. One of these should underlie data-gathering for at least some of the measures—tests, questionnaires, interviews, etc.—you intend to use.

In addition to the timing and placement of measures, the evaluation design prescribes who gets exposed to the program. In order to implement Designs 1 and 2, you will have to have some influence over whether students or other participants can be randomly assigned to programs. In order to implement Designs 3 or 5, you will have to find a non-randomized comparison group.

In short, for Designs 1, 2, 3, and 5, you will usually have to be in the position of planning the evaluation before the program gets underway. Since not every evaluator finds him- or herself in this position, Designs 4 and 6 are adequate where nothing else is possible.

Design 1: True Control Group

This design is ideal for choosing between Program X and another program since it measures exactly how Program X measures up against an alternative. The other program—Program C—might be a pre-existing program, or it might be a competitor or control program. Whatever the other program is, in order to implement this design, both Program X and Program C should be running at the same time.

Procedure

a. Identify all participants or groups who can get either Program X or Program C.

b. Pretest this group.

c. Randomly divide the individuals or groups of individuals into two groups, and give one group Program X and the other group Program C.

d. Make sure that:

- There is as little difference as possible in what happens to the two groups apart from the Program X/Program C difference—that is, avoid confounds.

- Program X and Program C stay distinct, not sharing or joining forces—that is, they avoid contamination.

e. Posttest both groups simultaneously.

Chapter 5, a Step-by-Step Guide for Conducting a Small Experiment, is an example of a True Control Group evaluation. If you choose either Design 1 or Design 2 for any of your measures, and if you can meet the preconditions listed in Step 1 on page 134 of Chapter 5, then use that step-by-step guide. Its prescription about how to evaluate is more detailed than this chapter's.

Design 2: True Control Group with Posttest Only

This design is identical to Design 1 except the pretest—Step b—is omitted. This design is useful when the experience of the pretest might itself interfere with program effects. This might be the case, for example, if a questionnaire were administered at the beginning of a program intended to change attitudes, thereby flagging for participants the program's intended effects. A pretest might also be unavailable or inconvenient to give.

Randomization in this design ensures equivalence of the groups receiving the two programs.

Design 3: Non-Equivalent Control Group

This is a good design for choosing between Program X and some other program, Program C, which will also be in operation during the period of the evaluation. As in Designs 1 and 2, Program C might be a control group or a competitor with Program X.

This design enables you to compare the results of Programs X and C on two groups which are similar even though they were not randomly assigned and are therefore not equivalent as in Designs 1 and 2.

Procedure

a. Find a similar group of participants who will be given Program C in the same time period that a group will be given Program X. How to Design a Program Evaluation gives suggestions for doing this.

b. Pretest both groups of individuals and collect information on both groups concerning characteristics which might affect their reactions to Programs X and C.

c. Investigate differences in what happens to the group getting Program X and the group getting Program C if these differences are likely to affect results.

d. Posttest both groups.

Design 4: Single Group Time Series

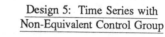

A series of measurements made during and/or after Program X gives a good picture of the impact of Program X on whatever is measured. This design requires scores collected from the same group on several occasions before Program X and on several occasions during and after Program X. The scores should be based on the same measuring instrument.

Design 5: Time Series with Non-Equivalent Control Group

This design involves making measurements exactly as in Design 4. But here, two groups of individuals are measured regularly: the group receiving Program X; and the other, a non-equivalent control group, not randomly assigned, like the one used in Design 3.

Design 6: Before-and-After Design (Allowing Informal Comparisons Only)

Design 1 and Design 2 are experimental designs because both Program X and a comparable or control program, C, are implemented to see which produces better results: a little experiment is run. If only Program X can be measured, then the only way to interpret the results of the measurements will be by comparing pretest and posttest results, or by making informal comparisons based on published data, school records, or predetermined standards. You might make one or all of the following comparisons:

☐ Comparisons of pretest and postest results for Program X.

☐ Comparison of Program X results with results from a national sample, the norm group for a standardized test. For example, in education, a national sample of students is used as a comparison group whenever you use results expressed as percentiles, grade equivalents, or stanines.

☐ Comparison of Program X results with results described in curriculum materials.

☐ Comparison of Program X results with results obtained by last year's participants.

☐ Comparison of Program X results with prespecified criteria; for example, "80% of students will achieve 75% of grade two math objectives." Such criteria may have been set up by staff, managers, the community, or the sponsor; or they may have been specified in a program plan.

Choose a sampling strategy for conducting data collection

Instructions

If either Program X or Program C is a large one with many participants at diverse sites, you will not be able to measure all the members of each group prescribed by your evaluation design or to look at implementation at every site. You will have to sample people to test, question, or observe, and possibly sites on which to focus as well. The number of sites and people you sample will depend on both available resources and on minimum requirements for validity and credibility.

Sampling plans for making data collection more manageable are discussed at several places in the kit. See How to Design a Program Evaluation, pages 161-165; How to Assess Program Implementation, pages 49 to 53; and How to Use Qualitative Methods in Evaluation, pages 51 to 60.

Choice of which sites to assess/observe depends on the questions you want to answer. If the program varies considerably from site to site, you should include in your selection representatives of each version of the program. This will be particularly crucial if you are exploring the relative effects of different planned or natural variations in the program. If the program is intended to be uniform across sites, choose sites based on other criteria such as the length of time the program has been in operation at the site, the amount of experience of teachers or staff, the characteristics of communities involved, or the amount of funds allotted to the program.

DECISION If you have been unable to obtain a comparison group, consider the possibility of using different versions of the program as Program X and Program C—perhaps the same program at qualitatively different sites.

CHECK Record your decisions:

☐ Program X sites will be sampled

Number of Program X sites to be sampled _____

On what basis? _____

_____

☐ Program C sites will be sampled

Number of Program C sites to be sampled _____

On what basis? _____

_____

☐ Programs X and C will represent different versions of the same program. These versions are:

- Program X sites _____

  Number of sites _____

- Program C sites _____

  Number of sites _____

☐ Programs X and C will represent the same program implemented at different sites:

- Program X sites have this characteristic

  _____

  Number of sites _____

- Program C sites have this characteristic

  _____

  Number of sites _____

NOTE In order to produce a representative description of the program, find out the optimal or most typical times to assess students/clients and others, question people, and observe program implementation at each site. Record these, and keep them in mind when scheduling the dates of data collection in Phase C, Step 1.

Instructions

If your activities will be financed from the program budget, you will have to determine early the financial boundaries of the service you provide. The cost of an evaluation is difficult to predict accurately. This is unfortunate, since what you will be able to promise the staff and planners will be determined by what you feel you can afford to do.

Estimate costs by getting the easy ones out of the way first. Find out costs per unit for each of these "fixed" expenses:

- ☐ Postage and shipping (bulk rate, parcel post, etc.) _____
- ☐ Photocopying and printing _____
- ☐ Travel and transportation _____
- ☐ Long-distance phone calls _____
- ☐ Test and instrument purchase _____
- ☐ Consultants _____
- ☐ Mechanical test or questionnaire scoring _____
- ☐ Data processing _____

These fixed costs will come "off the top" each time you sketch out the budget accompanying an alternative method for evaluating the program.

The most difficult cost to estimate is the most important one: the price of person-hours required for your services and those of the staff you assemble for the evaluation. If you are inexperienced, try to emulate other people. Ask how other evaluators estimate costs and then do likewise.

Develop a rule-of-thumb that computes the cost of each type of evaluation staff member per unit time period, such as "It costs $6,000 for one senior evaluator, working full time, per month." This figure should summarize all expenses of the evaluation, excluding only overhead costs unique to a particular study, such as travel and data analysis.

The staff cost per unit should include:

Salary of a staff member for that time unit

+ Benefits

+ Office and equipment rental

+ Secretarial and support services

+ Photocopying and duplicating

+ Telephone

+ Utilities

—> This equals the total routine expenses of running your office for the time unit in question, divided by the number of full-time evaluators working there.

Compute such a figure for each salary classification—Ph.D.'s, master's level staff, data gatherers, etc. Since the cost of each of these staff positions will differ, you can plan variously priced evaluations by juggling amounts of time to be spent on the evaluation by staff members in different salary brackets.

The tasks you promise to perform will in turn determine and be determined by the amount of time you can allot to the evaluation from different staff levels. An evaluation will cost more if it requires the attention of the most skilled and highly priced evaluators on your staff. This will be the case with studies requiring extensive planning, complicated analyses, and/or require sensitive qualitative analyses. Evaluations that use a simple design and routine data collection by graduate students or project staff will be correspondingly less costly.

 To estimate the cost of your evaluation, try these steps:

a. Do a task analysis of the tasks and resources required to complete your evaluation. Designate who is to be involved in each task and the amount of time required. Use a chart such as the following:

Task Analysis for Costing

| | Personnel Time Required (In hours or days) | | | | Other Special Costs (Service or materials purchased, travel, consultants, specialists, printing, mailing or communication) |
	Senior	Associate	Junior	Clerical/ Secretarial	

General Planning
Instrument Development
  Problem Simulation Test
    Specification
    Item Development
    Item Tryout
    . . .
 	
  Staff Questionnaire
  . . .
 	
Data Collection
  Problem Simulation Test
  Staff Questionnaire
 	
Data Analysis
  Problem Simulation Test
  Staff Questionnaire
  . . .
  Relationship between
    instruments
 	
Reporting
 	
TOTALS					

 To complete this task analysis, go back to the schedule you developed in Step 3.

b. Compute a cost-of-staff-per-unit-time figure for each job position occupied by someone who will work on the evaluation.

Depending on the amount of overhead staff support entered into the equation, this figure could be as high as twice the gross salary earned by a person in that position.

c. Compute the staff costs of the project by multiplying the cost-of-staff-per-unit-time figure by the total time estimated by Step **a** for each job position.

d. Compute the other special costs associated with the project.

The special costs will vary depending on the specific requirements of the project. These include such things as travel for data collection, test purchase or duplication, data coding services, computer services, mailing or shipping costs associated with data collection, consultant costs. The worksheets on the following pages may help you with your estimate.

Estimated Travel Costs

Task #	Destination/ Purpose	No. of People	No. of Trips	No. of Days	Air Fare	Ground Transportation	Per Diem Hotel & Meals	TOTAL
3	Data Collection	3	4	2	$200 x 3 people x 4 trips = 2400	$50 x 3 people x 4 trips = 600	$90 x 3 people x 2 days x 4 trips = 2160	5160

TOTAL: $_____

Estimated Consultant Costs

Task #	Consultant	Daily Fee	No. of Days	Total Fee	Travel Costs			TOTAL
					Air Fare	Ground Transp.	Per Diem	
5	Data Analyst	200	5	1000	500	50	3 x $90 = 270	1820

TOTAL: $_____

Other Special Costs

Special Printing:*

_____ Surveys x _____ pages each x # needed
     x $.___/page = _____

_____ Final Reports x _____ pages each
     x # copies = _____

Materials Purchase:

_____ Tests x $.___/each = _____

Mail:*

Mailing and return of surveys and other instruments
packages x _____ cost average each way
     x 2 = _____

Phone:

Long-distance calls for telephone surveys
_____ calls x $___ per call = _____

Computer:

Data entry _____
Computer time _____

*Be sure to include the extras you'll need for data
collection follow-ups.

---

observations. See if one or more of the following strategies
will reduce your requirement for expensive personnel time, or
trim some of the fixed costs.

☐ Sampling

☐ Employing junior staff members for some of the design, data-gathering, and report writing tasks

☐ Finding volunteer help, perhaps by persuading the staff
that you can supply richer and more varied information
or reach more sites if you have their cooperation

☐ Purchasing measures rather than designing your own

☐ Cutting planning time by building the evaluation on
procedures that you, or people whose expertise you can
easily tap, have used before

☐ Consolidating instruments and the times of their
administration

☐ Planning to look at different sites with different degrees
of thoroughness, concentrating your efforts on those
factors of greater importance

☐ Using paper-and-pencil instruments that can be machine
read and scored, where possible

☐ Relying more heavily on information that will be collected by others, such as state-administered tests and
records that are part of the program

e. Estimate the evaluation's total cost.

Total the costs estimated in c and d above. Add also your
indirect or overhead costs, if any. Compare this figure with
the amount you know to be already earmarked for the evaluation. If your budget is too high, consider whether funders
may be persuaded to increase the funding.

f. Trim, if necessary.

Rather than visiting an entire population of
program sites, for instance, visit a small
sample of them, perhaps one-third; send observers with checklists to a slightly larger
sample, and perhaps send questionnaires to the whole group
of sites to corroborate the findings from the visits and

Come to final agreement about services and responsibilities

Now that you've completed detailed planning, you can enter into a firm agreement with your sponsor. Your agreement could conform to the following format:

This agreement, made on _____, 19__ outlines the evaluation of the _____ project, funded by _____. The evaluation will take place from _____, 19__ to _____, 19__. The evaluator for this project is _____ assisted by _____ and _____ .

Focus of the Evaluation

The evaluation will address the following major questions or issues:

_____

_____

_____

In order to address these concerns, the evaluation will collect data on the following:

Program Outcomes: _____

_____

_____

Program Implementation: _____

_____

_____

Program Costs: _____

_____

_____

Other Factors: _____

_____

_____

Instrumentation

The evaluator will utilize a variety of sources of information:

Names of tests, if any, to be used: (Include what outcomes they address and any rationale you have for their selection) _____

_____

_____

Questionnaires to be developed or used:

_____

_____

Interviews: _____

_____

Observations: _____

_____

Data Collection Plans

Approximately _____ program and _____ control sites for data collection will be chosen. Of these, _____ will be studied intensively using a case study method; _____ will be examined by means of observation and interviews; and _____ will receive questionnaires or have records reviewed only. Testing will be conducted in _____ of these sites. Within each site, subjects will be sampled as follows:

_____

_____

_____

Staff members filling the following roles will be asked to cooperate: _____

_____

The schedule of data collection will be as follows:

_____

_____

Staff Participation

Staff members have agreed to cooperate with and assist data collection in the following ways: _____

_____

Approximately _____ meetings will be needed to report and describe the evaluation's findings. These meetings, scheduled to occur a few days after submission of interim reports, will be attended by people filling the following roles: _____

_____

The sponsors, planners, and/or staff have agreed that the following data will be made available:

_____

_____

Reporting

A draft report will be submitted _____. Following review by sponsors, _____ copies of the final version will be delivered by _____. Interim progress reports will be provided as follows: (as required)

_____

Budget

The evaluation as planned is anticipated to require the following expenditures:

Direct Salaries $_____

Evaluation and Assistant Benefits $_____

Other Direct Costs:

   Supplies and materials $_____

   Travel $_____

   Consultant services $_____

   Equipment rental $_____

   Communication $_____

   Printing and duplicating $_____

Data processing	$_____
Equipment purchase	$_____
Facility rental	$_____
Total Direct Costs	$_____
Indirect Costs	$_____
TOTAL COSTS	$_____

The contract outlined here prescribes the evaluation's general outline only. If you plan to describe either the program or the evaluation in greater detail, then include the description you formulated in Phase A. You may also want to provide additional detail on your design, sampling, and data collection approaches.

Collect and Analyze Information

At this point, the program evaluation has been thoroughly planned and is getting underway. The purpose of Phase C is to help you through the process of data collection and analysis. What remains is to see that everything proceeds as expected.

The steps in Phase C can be summarized as follows:

If you are conducting a qualitative study, Steps 3 and 4 will most likely be iterative.

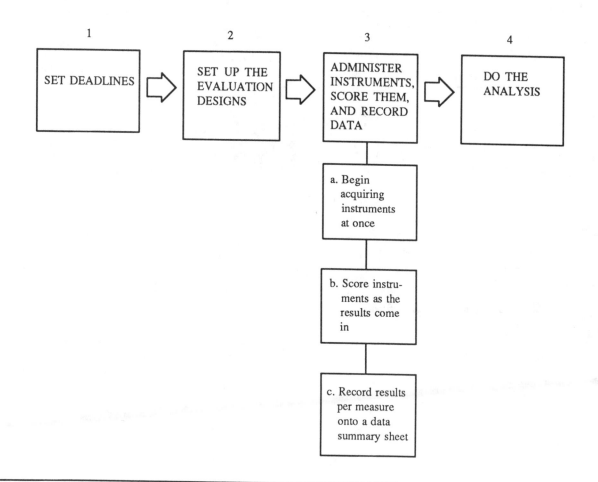

Instructions

If you are conducting a quantitative study, the following table should help you keep track of instrument development, administration, scoring, and data recording.

Instrument Use Table

1	2	3	4		5	6
Instrument	Completion deadline (if developed in-house)	Duplication/ receipt deadline	Administration deadlines		Scoring deadline	Coding or recording deadline
			pre	post		

Each of the How to books in the Program Evaluation Kit contains suggestions for administering the instruments you are using as well as detailed directions for recording, scoring, and summarizing their results.

Fill in deadlines for each phase of the instrument's use:

- Completed construction or receipt from a publisher
- Administration
- Scoring
- Recording of scores

A good rule-of-thumb to follow regarding deadlines is this:

- Start with the deadline for your evaluation report, and subtract three weeks. This is your latest possible deadline for coding or recording all data—Column 6. Make the deadline earlier if you think you will need more than three weeks to analyze data, draw charts and graphs, and write the final report. This, of course, will depend on the number of instruments you are using and the formality of your analysis and report.

- Set the scoring deadline in Column 5 according to the amount of help you will have and how much scoring is required. If your instruments are selected response and you are planning to have a service code the data (i.e., for computer entry), then they may be able to do it in a day or two if they have advance warning. If you or an assistant are going to do the scoring by hand, then more time may be required. If your instrument requires open-ended (e.g., essay) responses, be sure to include enough time to train your scorers thoroughly.

Be sure to allow time in your schedule to follow up on requests for instrument completion or other requests for data. This will help to ensure a better return rate.

The following should help you to schedule times for test administration, Column 4:

- The posttest should be given as near as possible to the end of the program to allow the program to have a maximum amount of time to work its effect. Do not, however, be alarmed if it turns out that you will need to give the posttest at a time when only 85% or so of the program time has elapsed—in early May, perhaps, for a program that runs the course of a school year. In most cases, the program will have had a chance to show its effect by then. Besides, it has been argued that testing in the last few weeks, or days, of a program, when people are unwinding for its termination, may actually reflect its effect less well than testing earlier. In other words, it is possible that program effects will peak at the point of about 85% to 95% elapsed time.

- Plan to postest well before the scoring deadline, particlarly if instruments must be sent away for scoring. For difficult-to-score tests, you might have to allow several weeks. Be mindful that when you have chosen to rely on statewide tests, you are at their mercy for receiving scores.

- The time of administration of the pretest should, in most cases, coincide with the beginning of the program. An exception to this is the situation in which the pretest is used as a basis for assigning students to programs via blocking or stratified sampling. If the pretest is to be used as a basis for assignment of students, then it should be given well before the program begins.

 How to Design a Program Evaluation, pages 35 to 45, contains additional details about when, how, and why to schedule pretests and posttests.

- With regard to the Completion/Receipt Deadline, Column 2, make sure that you schedule receipt of the instrument at least a week to 10 days before the administration deadline. This should allow for delays without seriously jeopardizing the rest of your schedule. Remember that constructing a test or questionnaire generally requires several drafts and tryouts.

 If you are using qualitative methods, the following table should help you monitor your schedule.

Source of Data	Initial Questtions/Issue Specifications Deadline	Site Entry Deadline	Data Collection Deadline

 How to Use Qualitative Methods in Evaluation contains guidelines on how to plan and schedule your efforts.

 If you are using a qualitative approach, your data collection efforts may well be iterative and certainly will be more fluid than quantitative approaches. You may complete a number of cycles of data collection and analysis prior to your final report. Be aware also that the time required for qualitative analysis is usually much greater than for quantitative analysis.

Set up the evaluation designs

In Phase B you selected data collection approaches and instruments with which to carry out your evaluation and you chose a design to determine when—and to whom—they would be administered. The purpose of this step is to help you ensure that the design is carried out.

Issues of design and random assignment are treated in depth in How to Design a Program Evaluation. In this book you will also find step-by-step directions for setting up any of the six designs you have chosen to use.

The three checklists which follow are intended to help you keep track of the implementation of the quantitative design you have chosen. Set up the checklist that is relevant to

your particular design. Use it to keep track of important information and to check the completion of activities essential to the design.

Checklist for a Control Group Design with Pretest—Designs 1, 2, and 3

1. Name the person responsible for setting up the design _____

If the design uses a true control group:

2. Will there be blocking? ☐ yes ☐ no

   (See How to Design a Program Evaluation, pages 150 to 154.)

3. If yes, based upon what?

   ☐ ability ☐ sex

   ☐ achievement ☐ other _____

4. Has randomization been completed?

   ☐ yes ☐ no Date _____

If the design uses a non-equivalent control group:

5. Name this group _____

6. List the major differences between the program and comparision groups—for example, sex, SES, ability, time of day in class, geographical location, age:

   _____

   _____

   _____

7. Has contact been made to secure the cooperation of the comparison group? ☐ yes Date _____

8. Agreement received from (Ms./Mr.) _____

9. Agreement was in the form of (letter/memo/personal conversation/etc.) _____

10. Confirmatory letter or memo sent? ☐ yes
    Date _____

11. Is there a list of students receiving the comparison program? ☐ yes ☐ no

    Where is it? _____

In either case:

12. Name of pretest _____

13. Pretest completed? ☐ yes Date _____

14. Staff or other program implementors warned:

    ☐ To avoid confounds? Memo sent or meeting held (date) _____

    ☐ To avoid contamination? Memo sent or meeting held (date) _____

    (See How to Design a Program Evaluation, page 63.)

15. List of possible confounds and contaminations

    _____

    _____

    _____

16. Check made that both programs will span the same
    time period? ☐   Date _____

17. Posttest given? ☐   Date _____

---

10. Confirmatory letter or memo sent? ☐
    Date _____

11. List of possible contaminations

    _____

    _____

    _____

Checklist for a Time Series Design with Optional Non-Equivalent Control Group —Designs 4 and 5

1. Name of person responsible for setting up and
   maintaining design _____

2. Names of instruments to be administered and
   readministered _____

   _____

3. Equivalent form of instruments to be:

   ☐ Made in-house?   ☐ Purchased?

4. Number of repeated measurements to be made per
   instrument _____

5. Dates of planned measurements:

   ☐ 1st _____   ☐ 5th _____
   ☐ 2nd _____   ☐ 6th _____
   ☐ 3rd _____   Additional:
   ☐ 4th _____   ☐ _____

If the design uses a control group:

6. Name of control group _____

7. List of major differences between the program group
   and the control group—for example, sex, SES,
   ability, geographical location, age

   _____

   _____

8. Contact made to secure cooperation of comparison
   group? ☐   Date _____

9. Agreement received from (Ms./Mr.) _____

Checklist for Before-and-After Design with Informal Comparison—Design 6

1. Name of person responsible for setting up the design

   _____

2. Comparison to be made between obtained posttest
   results and pretest results? ☐

   • Name(s) of instrument(s) to be used

     _____

     _____

   • Equivalent forms of instruments to be:

     ☐ Made   ☐ Purchased

   • List of participants receiving Form A on pretest and
     Form B on posttest

     _____

     _____

   • List of people receiving Form B on pretest and
     Form A on posttest _____

     _____

   • Dates of planned measurements:

     Pretest _____   Completed? ☐
     Posttest _____   Completed? ☐

3. Comparison to be made via standardized tests? ☐

   • Name of standardized test(s) _____

     _____

   • Test given? ☐   Date _____

   • Scoring and ranking of program students com-
     pleted? ☐   Date _____

4. Comparison to be made between obtained results and
   results described in curriculum materials? ☐

   • Name of curriculum materials _____

     _____

- Unit test results collected and filed? ☐

- Unit test results from program graphed or otherwise compared with norm group? ☐

5. Comparison to be made between results from a previous year and the results of the program group? ☐

   - Which results from last year will be used—for example, grades, districtwide tests?

   _____

   - Last year's results tabulated and graphed? ☐

   - List made of possible differences between this and last year's (or last time's) group that might differentially affect results? ☐

   _____

   _____

   _____

   - Program X's results collected? ☐

   - Program X's results scored and graphed, or otherwise compared, with last year's? ☐

6. Comparison to be made between obtained results and prespecified criteria about attainment of program objectives? ☐

   - Whose criteria are these—for example, staff, district, board, program developers?

   _____

   - State the criteria to be met _____

   _____

   _____

   - Objectives-based test results collected and filed? ☐

   - Objectives-based test results graphed, or otherwise compared, with criterion? ☐

Sampling Plan Checklist

1. The sample will ensure adequate representation to different types of:

   ☐ Sites—what kinds? _____

   ☐ Time periods—which ones? _____

   ☐ Program units or components —which ones? _____

   ☐ Program roles—which ones? _____

   ☐ Participant characteristics—name them

   _____

   ☐ Other _____

2. The sampling plan comprises a matrix or cube with _____ cells (see How to Assess Program Implementation, pages 52 to 53).

3. How many cases will be sampled from each cell? _____ (See How to Design a Program Evaluation, pages 161-165, for suggestions about selecting random samples.)

4. Cases selected? ☐

5. For each time selected:

   - Have instruments been administered? ☐

     Comments _____

   - What deviations from the sampling plan have occurred? _____

   _____

NOTE If your approach is primarily qualitative, see How to Use Qualitative Methods in Evaluation, Chapter 3, for a description of the critical design and sampling requirements you will need to ensure.

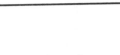 If you have chosen to administer instruments at only a sample of program sites or to a sample of respondents, then use the following table to keep track of the proper implementation of your sampling plan.

Administer instruments, score them, and record data

Instructions

a. Once you have decided which instruments to use, begin acquiring them at once. Have no illusions—ordering and constructing instruments will take a long time, possibly months.

 If you intend to buy instruments, use the form letters in the various How to books for ordering them. Check the list of test publishers in the How to books for sources of published tests.

 If you plan to construct your own instruments, write a memo to those in charge of producing them, leaving no doubt about who is responsible and deadlines for their completion.

 Instruments made in-house must be tried out, debugged, and evaluated for technical quality. To aid the process, the kit's measurement books discuss reliability and validity as they apply to the three primary measurement concerns treated in the books (see Performance, Chapter 5, Attitudes, Chapter 11, Implementation, Chapter 3, and Qualitative Methods, Chapter 2). A little run-through with a few participants might mean the difference between a mediocre instrument and a really excellent one.

 Keep tabs on instrument orders. If you have not received them within two weeks of the deadline, prod the publisher or your in-house developer.

 Once each instrument is completed or received, plan how it will be scored and recorded.

b. Score instruments as the results come in.

If the instrument has a selected response format—for instance, multiple-choice, true-false, Likert-scale—make sure you have a scoring key or template. If it has an open-ended format, make sure you have a set of correctness criteria for scoring, or a way of categorizing and coding questionnaire or interview responses.

 See How to Assess Program Implementation, pages 120-121; How to Measure Attitudes, pages 159-169, and 170-171; and How to Measure Performance and Use Tests, pages122-125. These sections contain information about scoring or coding open-response items, essays, and reports. If the test is to be scored elsewhere by a state or district office or by an agency with whom you have a contract for testing and scoring, and you are to receive a printout of the results, decide whether you wish to score sections of it for your own purposes. In some cases, achievement of objectives can be measured via partial scoring of a standardized test.

 See How to Use Qualitative Methods, Chapter 6 for how to code qualitative data.

c. Have data computer-coded or record results per measure onto a data summary sheet.

 Once you know what the scores from your instruments will look like, decide whether you want results for each examinee, mean results for each class, or percentage results for each item. Then, when each instrument has been administered, score and code the instruments as soon as possible.

 Once scoring is completed, consult the appropriate How to books for suggestions about formatting and filling out data summary sheets. See How to Measure Attitudes, pp. 160-165 ; How to Assess Program Implementation, pages 122-123; and How to Measure Performance and Use Tests, pages 125-151.

Construct separate files or data summary sheets for Program X people and the comparison group so that it is impossible to get them confused. Then delegate the scoring and recording tasks.

When each graph and statistical test is completed, examine it carefully and write a one-or-two sentence description that summarizes your conclusions from reading the graph and noting the results of the analysis.

Save the graphs and summary sentences that seem to you to give the clearest picture of the program's impact. These can be used as a basis for the Results section of your report.

_____

_____

_____

_____

_____

_____

_____

_____

_____

Graphs—even rough ones—are great aids to data analyses; they allow you to easily look for trends and regularities in your results. At times the graph, if it shows a glaringly clear trend, will be all you need to support your report conclusions.

The How to books concerned with measuring attitudes, performance, and program implementation describe graphing methods for scores obtained from every type of instrument described in the kit. Graphs are also discussed in Chapter 3 of How to Communicate Evaluation Findings, and Chapter 2 , How to Analyze Data.

You should graph results even when all you intend to report is average scores per group—for instance, "The average reading score for Program X was 10 raw score points higher than for Program C." In these cases, graph the average scores per group, according to characteristics such as grade level, sex, SES, or ability. Graphing will help you uncover much information that you did not know you had.

So, for each instrument administered, plan to produce at least one graph.

For qualitative studies, How to Use Qualitative Methods in Evaluation details analyses procedures for identifying key issues and trends, and for aggregating and summarizing data.

Do the analysis

For quantitative studies, How to Analyze Data details procedures for summarizing scores through indicators of central tendency, such as the mean, and indicators of score variability, such as the standard deviation; performing tests for statistical significance; and calculating measures of relationship such as correlations. For more complex analyses, consult a data analyst.

You do not have to do statistical tests to produce a good report. However, doing them will make your conclusions stronger.

How to Analyze Data describes statistical tests that can be performed by anyone who can multiply and divide. Don't decide against performing statistics because you think it will be too complex.

Whether or not you can perform statistical tests depends on the design of the evaluation and the measurements you made. If you have used one of the group comparison designs—Designs 1, 2, 3, and 5—you can perform statistical tests that show the significance of the difference between the scores of the two groups, that is, whether the difference could have occurred by chance. If you are using Design 6, you can do a statistical test only under these circumstances:

• If you are comparing performance of the program group on a standardized test with that of the test's norm group and the standard deviation of that group's scores is available, or

• If your reference group is last year's or last time's group, or you are comparing pretest and posttest results for the same group.

How to Design a Program Evaluation discusses these situations in greater detail.

As a general rule, if you can calculate an average score per participant or an average response per question, and if you can compare this average for one group (say, Program X) with the average from another group (Program C), then you can do a statistical test.

If you are using mechanical scoring or data processing, then set up the appropriate data files and proceed with the analysis.

A table like the one below will help you keep track of data analysis:

Data Analysis Table

1 Instrument	2 Statistical analysis to be done	3 Will results be graphed?	4 Graph format chosen—refer to page xx in How to book

List instruments you have scored in Column 1. Then, consult the How to book most closely related to each instrument, design, or analysis, and follow its suggestions concerning graphing. Mark your decision about whether or not to graph in Column 3 and indicate the graph format to be used—you might even sketch this—in Column 4.

In Column 2, list the statistical analyses—tests for significance, correlations, etc.—to be performed.

Instructions

If you have fairly faithfully followed this Step-by-Step Guide in designing and carrying out your evaluation, then by now you are well prepared for presenting the final report. The logic and sequence of this guide is the same as that to be followed in a final report. All that remains now is for you to put what has been recorded on the worksheets suggested in this chapter into a coherent form for your audience.

There are three steps in Phase D:

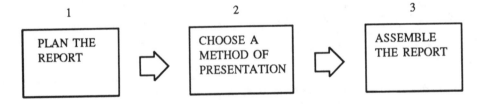

1.
PLAN THE REPORT

2.
CHOOSE A METHOD OF PRESENTATION

3.
ASSEMBLE THE REPORT

Instructions

<u>How to Communicate Evaluation Findings</u> gives section-by-section directions for preparing formal and informal reports for many different audiences. Read Chapter 2 and look over the outline in Chapter 4 to help you decide which of the topics apply to your report. If you will need to describe program implementation, look at the report outline in Chapter 7 of <u>How to Assess Program Implementation.</u> Then write a quick general outline of what you plan to discuss.

Instructions

Decide whether your report to each primary user will be oral or written, formal or informal.

Chapter 2 of <u>How to Communicate Evaluation Findings</u> lists a set of pointers to help you organize what you intend to say and to decide how best to say it.

Assemble the report

Instructions

A worksheet like the one below will help you to record your decisions about reporting and to keep track of the progress of your report.

Final Report Preparation Worksheet

1. List the audiences to receive each report, date reports are due, and type of report to be given to each audience. Some reports may be suitable for more than one audience.

Audience	Date Report Due
_____	_____
_____	_____
_____	_____

2. How many different reports will you have to prepare?

   _____

3. For each different report you submit, complete this section:

   Report #1   Audience(s) _____

   Checklist for Preparing Evaluation Report:

   - Report will be: ☐ formal   ☐ informal
                     ☐ oral   ☐ written

   - Deadline for review draft _____
     Completed? ☐

   - Deadline for final draft _____
     Completed? ☐

   - Deadline for finished audiovisuals, if any _____
     Completed? ☐

- Deadline for finished tables and graphs

  _____

  Completed? ☐

- Names of proofreaders of final draft, audiovisuals, or tables

  _____

  Contacted and agreement made? ☐

  _____

  Contacted and agreement made? ☐

  _____

  Contacted and agreement made? ☐

- Date agreed upon as deadline for getting drafts to proofreaders. These are absolute deadlines for completing drafts:

  Draft sent? _____   ☐
  Draft sent? _____   ☐
  Draft sent? _____   ☐

- Dates drafts must be received in order to revise in time for final report deadlines?

  _____ Proofread draft received? ☐
  _____ Proofread draft received? ☐
  _____ Proofread draft received? ☐

This is the end of the Step-by-Step Guides for Conducting a Summative Evaluation. By now evaluation is a familiar topic to you and, we hope, a growing interest. This guide is designed to be used again and again. Perhaps you will want to use it in the future, each time trying a more elaborate design and more sophisticated measures. Evaluation is a new field. Be assured that people evaluating programs—yourself included—are breaking new ground.

Chapter 5
Step-by-Step Guide for Conducting a Small Experiment

The self-contained guide which constitutes this chapter will be useful if you need a quick but powerful pilot test—or a whole evaluation—of *a definable short-term program or program component*. The guide provides start-to-finish instructions and an appendix containing a sample evaluation report (Appendix A). This step-by-step guide is particularly appropriate for evaluators who wish to assess the effectiveness of *specific materials, services, and/or activities* aimed at accomplishing a *few specific objectives*.

If a major purpose of the program you are evaluating is to produce achievement or performance results, this guide outlines *an ideal way to find out how good these results are: conduct an experiment*. For a period of days, weeks, or months, give participants (clients, students, patients) the program or program component you wish to evaluate while an equivalent group, a *control or comparison* group, does not receive it. Then at the end of the period test both groups. This step-by-step guide shows you how to conduct such an evaluation.

Whenever possible, the step-by-step guide uses checklists and worksheets to help you keep track of what you have decided and found out. Actually, the worksheets might be better called "guidesheets" since you will have to copy many of them onto your own paper rather than use the one in the book. Space simply does not permit the book to provide places to list large quantities of data.

As you use the guide, you will come upon references marked by the symbol ◪. These direct you to read sections of various *How to* books contained in the *Program Evaluation Kit*. At these junctures in the evaluation, it will be necessary for you to review a concept or follow a procedure outlined in one of the kit's eight resource books:

- *How to Focus an Evaluation*
- *How to Design a Program Evaluation*
- *How to Use Qualitative Methods in Evaluation*
- *How to Assess Program Implementation*
- *How to Measure Attitudes*
- *How to Measure Performance and Use Tests*
- *How to Analyze Data*
- *How to Communicate Evaluation Findings*

Should You Be Using This Step-by-Step Guide?

The appropriateness of this guide depends on whether or not you will be able to set up certain *preconditions* to make the evaluation possible. Check each of the preconditions listed in Step 1. If you can arrange to meet *all* of them, then you can use the evaluation strategy presented in this guide. As you assess the preconditions, you will be taking the first step in planning the evaluation. This step-by-step guide lists 13 steps in all. A flowchart showing relationships among these steps appears in Figure 5. You may wish to check off the steps as they are accomplished.

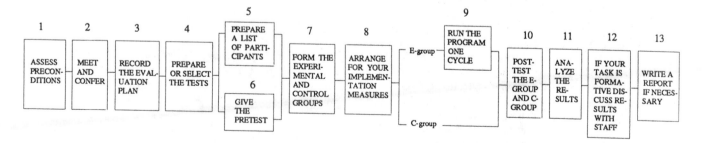

Figure 5. The steps for accomplishing a small experiment listed in this guide

Assess preconditions

Instructions

Put a check in each box if the precondition can be met. For the first three preconditions, there are some decisions to be recorded on the lines provided. Record these decisions in pencil since you may change them later. This step-by-step guide will be useful to you only if you can meet all five preconditions.

☐ PRECONDITION 1. An outcome measure will be available.

A test can be made or selected to measure what participants are supposed to learn from the program or how they are supposed to change. Write down what the outcome measure(s) will probably be:

_____

_____

_____

☐ PRECONDITION 2. A sample of cases* can be defined.

You can list at least 20, say, participants for whom this program would be suitable and for whom, therefore, the outcome measure is an appropriate test of what they acquired in the program. Write down the criteria that will be used to select participants for the sample:

_____

_____

_____

*A case is an entity producing a score on the outcome measure. In educational programs the cases of interest are nearly always students—though they could be classrooms, school districts, other groupings. In social service programs, cases of interest often are clients or other service recipients; in other programs, cases of interest may be patients, residents, employees, salespeople, etc. The word participant is used throughout the guide to describe the relevant case of interest.

☐ PRECONDITION 3. A time period—a cycle—can be identified.

You can identify a time period which is of a duration appropriate to acquire the skills the outcome measure taps. Call this period of time one cycle of the program. Write down what length of time one cycle of the program will probably last:

_____

_____

_____

☐ PRECONDITION 4. An experimental group and a control group or comparison group can be set up.

For one cycle at least, one group of participants in the sample will get the program and another will not. The latter group may receive no program or may participate in a competing alternative. If the program can run through several cycles, having a "no program" group does not mean that some participants will never get the program, just that they must wait their turn. In this way, no participants are left out—a concern which sometimes makes people unwilling to run an experiment.

☐ PRECONDITION 5. Participants who are to get the program can be randomly selected.

The students who are to get the program during the experimental cycle will be randomly selected from the sample.

If each of the five preconditions listed above can be met, then you will be able to run a true experiment. This is the best test you can make of the effectiveness of the program or program component for producing measurable results.

This step helps you work out a number of practical details that must be settled before you can complete your plans for the pilot test or evaluation.

You will need to meet and confer with the people whose cooperation you need and, possibly, with members of other evaluation audiences. You will need to reach agreement with them about:

- [ ] How the study should be run
- [ ] How to identify participants for the program
- [ ] What program the control group should receive
- [ ] The appropriate outcome measure
- [ ] Whether to use additional measures
- [ ] What procedures will be used to measure implementation
- [ ] To whom results will be reported—and how

How Should the Study Be Run?

In particular, are participants to receive the program in addition to the regular program or instead of the regular program? If the program is to be used in addition to the regular program, participants will have to be scheduled for the new program sometime other than the regular program period. A means of scheduling will need to be agreed upon.

How Should Participants Be Identified for the Sample?

It might be that the sample will simply be all the individuals in a certain unit (class/community/office). On the other hand, perhaps the program is intended only for participants who have a certain need or meet some criterion. In this case, you will need to agree upon clear selection criteria.

If the program is remedial, selection might be based on low scores on a pretest, or you might use staff nominations. Test scores for selection are preferred if the outcome measure is to be a test. The problem with basing selection on an existing set of test scores is that they might be incomplete; scores might be missing for some participants. You could use the outcome measure as a selection pretest.

How to Design a Program Evaluation, pages 37 and 38, discusses selection tests. See also How to Measure Performance and Use Tests, pages 130-131.

How many participants will you need? The more the better, but certainly you should avoid ending up with fewer than six pairs of participants, a total of 12. If during the program cycle, one participant in a pair is absent too often or fails to take the posttest, the pair will have to be dropped from the analysis. The longer the cycle, the more likely it is that you will lose pairs in this way. Bearing this in mind, be sure to select a large enough sample. If it looks as if the sample will be too small—perhaps because the program has limited materials—you should abandon an experimental test or run the experiment several times with different groups each time and then combine results to perform a single analysis.

What Program Should the Control Group Receive?

If one group of participants will get the program and a control group will not, the question arises about exactly what should happen to the control group. Should the control group receive no program? Should they receive the old/existing program, or should they receive another competing program?

It is best to set up the experiment to match the way in which the program will be used in the future. If the program will be used as an adjunct to a regular program, then set up the experiment so that the experimental group gets the program in addition to the regular program. If the program, on the other hand, is a replacement for an existing program, then the control group will get the existing program and the experimental group will get only the new program. If you are interested in assessing the effectiveness of two separate programs, either of which might replace the regular one, then give one to the experimental group and one to the control.

 How to Design a Program Evaluation discusses on pages 26 to 35 what should happen to control groups.

What Outcome Measure—Posttest—Is Reasonable for Detecting the Effect of One Cycle of the Experiment?

 The posttest must meet the requirements of a good test. It should therefore be:

- Representative of all the relevant objectives of the program
- Sufficiently long to ensure good reliability
- Clearly understandable to the participants
- Supported by data about its reliability and validity

 A good posttest is essential. Whether you plan to purchase it or construct it yourself, refer to How to Measure Performance and Use Tests.

Do You Need Other Measures in Addition to the Outcome Measure?

 Will the posttest provide a sufficient basis on which to judge the program? If the posttest contains many items which reflect specific details of the program—special vocabulary, for instance, or performance problems that use only a particular format—then a high posttest score may not represent much growth in general skills, if this is a program interest. In such a case, you might want to use an additional posttest for measuring achievement that contains more general items.

Since an immediate posttest will measure the initial impact of a program, you may wish to measure retention by administering another test some time later. You may, in addition, need to measure other program outcomes such as the attitudes of participants, staff, or others.

 See How to Measure Performance and Use Tests and How to Measure Attitudes.

What Procedures Will Be Used for Measuring Program Implementation?

 As the program runs through a cycle, a record should be kept of which participants actually participated in the program and which participants did not, perhaps because of absences. You must also keep careful track of what the experiences of program and control participants looked like.

 See How to Assess Program Implementation.

Which People Will Be the Primary Users? Which Other Audiences will be Informed?

 Check primary and secondary users by marking "1" or "2" as relevant

- ☐ Staff
- ☐ The program's planners and designers
- ☐ Local managers or administrators
- ☐ District or regional personnel
- ☐ Board members or other policymakers
- ☐ Community groups
- ☐ State groups
- ☐ The media
- ☐ Union organizations

Do meetings need to be held with any of these groups, either to give information or to hear their concerns, or for both reasons?

☐ Yes   ☐ No

If yes, hold such meetings.

 You and the others involved have now finished deciding how to do the evaluation. Once these decisions are firm, go back to Step 1 and change the preconditions entries you made there if necessary.

Record the evaluation plan

Instructions

Construct and complete a worksheet like the one below, summarizing the decisions made during Step 2. Contents of the worksheet can be used later as a first draft of parts of the evaluation report.

If <u>two</u> programs or components are being compared, and each is equally likely to be adopted, then you will have to carefully describe <u>both</u>.

PROGRAM DESCRIPTION WORKSHEET

This worksheet is written in the past tense so that when you have completed it you will have a first draft of two sections to your report: those that described the program and the evaluation. For more specific help with deciding what to say, consult How to Communicate Evaluation Findings.

Background Information About the Program

A. Origin of the Program

_____

_____

B. Goals of the Program

_____

_____

_____

C. Characteristics of the Program—materials, activities, services, and administrative arrangements

_____

_____

_____

_____

_____

D. Participants Involved in the Program

_____

_____

_____

E. Staff and Others Involved in the Program

_____

_____

_____

Purpose of the Evaluation Study

A. Purposes of the Evaluation

_____

_____

_____

_____

_____

_____

_____

_____

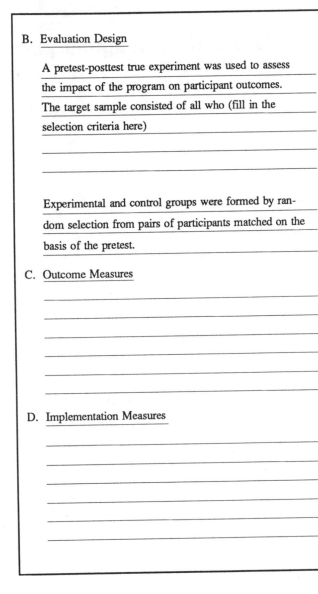

B. Evaluation Design

A pretest-posttest true experiment was used to assess
the impact of the program on participant outcomes.
The target sample consisted of all who (fill in the
selection criteria here)

Experimental and control groups were formed by random selection from pairs of participants matched on the
basis of the pretest.

C. Outcome Measures

D. Implementation Measures

Once you have completed the worksheet, you have prepared
descriptions of the program and of the evaluation. These descriptions will serve as your first draft of the evaluation
report.

Prepare or select the tests

Instructions

The Pretest

Use one of three kinds of pretests:

- A test to identify the sample of participants eligible for the program—this is a <u>selection test</u>

- A test of ability or predispositions given because you believe these will affect results, and you therefore want the average abilities or predispositions of the experimental and control or comparison groups to be roughly equal

- A pretest which is the same as the posttest, or its equivalent, so that you can be sure that the posttest shows a gain in knowledge or skill that was not there before

In most cases, it is desirable that the pretest should be an alternate, parallel form of the posttest or of the performance measure itself. If this will be possible in your situation, then produce a thorough test which will be used as both pretest and posttest.

Preparing the Pretest Yourself

 <u>How to Measure Performance and Use Tests</u>, Chapter 4, lists resources, item banks, and guides to help you construct a test yourself. <u>How to Measure Attitudes</u> gives step-by-step directions for constructing attitude measures of all sorts.

Once the test has been written, try it out with a small sample of participants to ensure that it is understandable and that it yields an appropriate pattern of scores for a pretest—not too many high scores so that there is room at the top for students to show growth. The tryout participants should <u>not</u> be those who will be assigned to either the experimental or control groups. You will need at least five participants for the tryout. They should be as similar as possible to the individuals who are to receive the program.

 Check off these substeps in test development as you accomplish them:

- [ ] Test or other performance measure has been drafted or selected

- [ ] Test or measure has been tried out with a small group of participants

- [ ] Results of the tryout have been graphed and examined. Consult Chapter 2 of <u>How to Analyze Data</u> for help with graphing scores.

- [ ] Test or measure has been revised, if necessary

- [ ] Test or other necessary materials have been reproduced in quantity ready for use

 If you intend to use the pretest you have purchased or written for <u>selection</u> of participants, then you will, of course, have to administer the test <u>before</u> you decide which participants are eligible. In this case, complete Step 6 before Step 5.

If the pretest will be administered to program and control groups <u>after</u> the groups have been formed, then go on next to Step 5.

Prepare a list of participants

Instructions

 List all participants for whom one cycle of the program will be appropriate. In order to construct this list, you must have a set of criteria for selection. These should have been established in Step 1 and recorded on the worksheet in Step 3.

Write the names of the participants who meet the selection criteria down the left-hand side of the paper. Call this a sample list.

If you are using the selection test as a pretest as well, list students in order by score, from highest to lowest, and record each student's score next to his or her name.

If you are doing your analyses by computer, assign each participant a unique ID number.

Your Sample List might look like this:

SAMPLE LIST	
Adams, Jane	01
Bellows, John	02
Cartwright, Jack	03
Dayton, Maurice	04
Dearborn, Fred	05
Eaton, Susie	06
James, Alice	07
Markham, Mark	08
Payne, Tom	09
Pine, Judy	10
Taylor, Harvey	11
Vine, Grace	12
Washington, Roger	13
Williams, Greg	14

Give the pretest

Instructions

Where possible, it is preferable to give the pretest at one sitting to all participants concerned. Be sure no copies of the test are lost. All tests handed out must be returned at the end of the testing period. For obvious reasons, this is critical if the test will be used again as a posttest.

Tests are more likely to get lost when they use a separate answer sheet which is also collected separately. If your test uses a separate answer sheet, then have students place answer sheets inside the test booklet, and collect the two together.

If your pre-measure is not a test but rather another kind of program indicator, e.g., absence rate, frequency of disturbance, health habits, sales productivity, or some other measure of participants' relevant predisposition, gather these data now.

Instructions

a. Record pretest scores or other pre-program indicators on the sample list if you have not already done so.

b. Graph the pretest or other indicator scores.

See Worksheets 2A-2B of How to Analyze Data for help with this step.

Are the scores appropriate for a pretest? That is, are scores relatively spread out with few students achieving the maximum or are they uniformly low? If yes, continue.

If the test was too easy, prepare and give another test with more difficult items. The program's objectives and plans might need revision too if a reliable test that was well matched to the program's objectives was too easy for the target participants.

c. Rank order the participants according to pretest or other indicator scores.

If it is not already arranged according to student scores, rewrite the sample list starting with the student with the highest score and working down to the lowest.

d. Form "matched" pairs.

Draw a line under the top two participants, the next two, and so on.

Bellows	38
Eaton	36
Adams	35
Dayton	35
James	35
Payne	32
Dearborn	31
Vine	30

e. From each pair, randomly assign one participant to the experimental group and the other participant to the control or comparison group.

To accomplish the random assignment, toss a coin. Call the experimental group or E-group "heads" and the control or C-group "tails." If a toss for the first person in the first pair gives you heads, assign this person to the E-group by putting an E by his name. His match, the other person in the pair, is then assigned to the C-group. If you get tails, the first person in the pair goes to the C-group and the other to the E-group.

Repeat the coin toss for each pair, assigning the first person according to the coin toss and his match to the other group. If there is an odd number of students, just randomly assign the odd student to one or the other group, but do not count him in the analysis later.

f. If you are doing your analyses by hand, prepare a data sheet.

Have a list of the E-group and C-group students typed on a Data Sheet. This sheet should place the E-group at the left-hand side with a column for the posttest scores, then the C-group and the score column at the right. Always keep matched pairs on the same row. Columns 5, 6, and 7 will contain calculations to be performed later.

Data Sheet

1	2	3	4	5	6	7
E-Group	Post-test	C-Group	Post-test	d	$(d-\bar{d})$	$(d-\bar{d})^2$

g. If you are doing your analyses by computer, prepare a roster for data entry.

Sample Directions for Data Roster

Column #	Content
1-2	Student ID#
3	Experimental or Control Group (1 = E; 2 = C)
4-5	Pretest Score
6-7	Posttest Score
. . .	Other measures

Step 8

Arrange for your implementation measures

Instructions

Ensure that the program has been implemented as planned. This means ensuring that the students who are supposed to get the program (the E-group) do get it, and the others (the C-group) get what they are supposed to—either no program, the regular program, or a competing alternative.

To accomplish this, try the following:

- Work closely with staff to ensure that the program groups receive the program at the appropriate times. Arrange a plan for carefully monitoring participant absences from the program.

- Set up a record-keeping system to verify implementation of the program. For example, participants could sign a log book as they arrive for the program, or perhaps they could

turn in their work after each session. In addition, if possible, plan to have observers record whether the program in action looks the way it has been described.

Refer back to the worksheet in Step 3 (Implementation Measures) to review your decisions on how to measure program implementation.

Check How to Assess Program Implementation for suggestions about collecting information to describe the program.

Run the program one cycle

Instructions

Let the program run as naturally as possible, but check that accurate records are kept of the participants' exposure to the program.

 Be careful. If staff or the evaluator pay extra attention to the experimental group, this alone could cause positive outcomes. So be as unobtrusive as possible.

Step 10

Posttest the E-group and C-group

Instructions

Give the posttest to the experimental and control participants at one sitting, if possible, so that testing conditions are the same for all. If one sitting is not possible, standardize all the conditions surrounding test administration and try to give the test to all groups during the same time period.

Of course, some of your outcome measures might not be tests as such. Interviews, observations, or whatever, should also be obtained from the experimental and control groups under conditions that are as similar as possible.

If necessary, schedule make-up tests for participants absent from the posttest.

a. Score the posttests.

If the test you have constructed yourself contains closed response items—for example, multiple choice, true-false—then you can delegate someone to score the tests for you.

 How to Measure Performance and Use Tests, pages 122-125, contains suggestions for scoring and recording results from your own tests.

b. Check the data set and prune as necessary.

Use the Sample List (Step 5) to complete this procedure.

Check for absences from the program. If some participants in either the experimental or control group missed a lot of the program, they should be dropped from the sample. You and your primary user will have to agree about how many absences will require dropping a participant from the analysis. One day's absence in a cycle of one week would probably be significant since it represents 20% of program time. A week's absence in a six month program, on the other hand, could probably be ignored.

If you decide that participants in the experimental group should be dropped from the analysis if their absences exceeded, say, six days during the program, then control group participants absent six or more days should also be dropped. This keeps the two groups comparable in composition. If the control group received a program representing a critical competitor to the program in question, then control group absences should be noted as well and the Sample List pruned accordingly.

 From attendance records, determine the number of days each participant was absent during the program cycle. Record this information in appropriately labeled columns added to the Sample List. Drop all participants whose absences exceeded a tolerable amount for inclusion in the experiment. For every participant dropped, the corresponding control group match will have to be dropped also. Drop as well any participant for whom there is no posttest score, and drop that participant's match also.

c. Summarize attrition.

Summarize results from pruning of the data in the table below. The number dropped from each group is called its "mortality" or "attrition."

TABLE OF ATTRITION DATA

Number of Participants Remaining in the Study
After Attrition for Various Reasons

	Experimental Group	Control Group
Number assigned on basis of pretest		
Number dropped because of excessive absence from program		
Number dropped because of lack of posttest score		
Number dropped because match was dropped		
Number retained for analysis		

d. Record posttest scores on the data sheet for participants who have remained in the analysis.

e. Test to see if the difference in posttest scores is significant.

Were you to record just any two sets of posttest scores, it is likely that one of the groups would have higher scores than the other just by chance. What you now need to ask is whether the difference you will almost inevitably find between the E- and C-group posttest scores is so slight that it could have occurred by chance alone.

 The logic underlying tests of statistical significance is described in <u>How to Analyze Data</u>. In fact, pages 64-69 of that book discuss the t-test for matched groups, to be used here, in detail.

To decide whether one or the other has scored significantly higher in this situation, <u>you will use a correlated t-test</u>—correlated because of the matched pairs used to form the two groups. Using your data, you will calculate a statistic, t. You will then compare this <u>obtained value of t with values in a table</u>. If your obtained value is bigger than the one in the table, the <u>tabled t-value</u>, then you can reject the idea that the results were just due to chance. You will have a statistically significant result. Below are the steps for completing this procedure by hand. You may prefer, of course, to use a statistical package on the computer.

Steps for Calculating and Testing t

Calculate t

This is the formula for t:

$$t = \frac{(\bar{d})\,(\sqrt{n})}{s_d}$$

In order to calculate it, you need to first compute the three quantities in the formula:

$\bar{d}$ = average difference score

$\sqrt{n}$ = the square root of the number of matched pairs

s_d = the standard deviation of the difference scores

Use the Data Sheet from Step 7 to help you calculate quantities for the t equation.

Data Sheet

1	2	3	4	5	6	7
E-Group	Post-test	C-Group	Post-test	d	$(d-\bar{d})$	$(d-\bar{d})^2$

Page 151 shows a Data Sheet that has been computed.

To compute $\bar{d}$. First find the difference between the scores on the posttests for each pair of participants. The difference, d, for a pair is the quantity:

Note that whenever a C-group participant has scored higher than an E-group participant, the difference is a negative number. Record these differences in Column 5 of the Data Sheet.

Then add up the entries in Column 5 and divide that sum by the number of pairs being used in the analysis, n. This gives you the average difference between the E-group and C-group. Call it $\bar{d}$, read "d bar."

 = $\bar{d}$

To compute s_d. Fill in the quantities for Columns 6 and 7. For Column 6, subtract from each value in Column 5, and record the result. For Column 7, square each number in Column 6 and divide their sum by n-1, the number that is one less than the number of pairs. Take the square root of your last answer and record this below as s_d .

 = s_d

To compute $\sqrt{n}$. Take the square root of the number of matched pairs—not the number of participants—which you are using in the analysis. This $\sqrt{n}$. Enter it here:

= $\sqrt{n}$

To compute t. Now enter these values in the formulas for t below:

$$t = \frac{(\bar{d})\,(\sqrt{n})}{s_d}$$

Multiply the top line. Then divide the result by s_d to get your t-value. Enter it here:

 = obtained t-value

Find the tabled t-value

Using the table below, go down the left-hand column until you reach the number which is equal to the <u>number of</u> <u>matched pairs</u> you were analyzing. Be careful to use the <u>number of pairs</u>, not the number of participants.

Table of t-Values for Correlated Means

Number of matched pairs	Tabled t-value for a 10% probability (one-tailed test)
6	1.48
7	1.44
8	1.41
9	1.40
10	1.38
11	1.37
12	1.36
13	1.36
14	1.35
15	1.34
16	1.34
17	1.33
18	1.33
19	1.32
20	1.32
21	1.32
22	1.32
23	1.32
24	1.32
25	1.31
26	1.31
•	•
40	1.30
•	•
120	1.29

The t-value in the left-hand column that corresponds to the number of <u>matched pairs</u> is your tabled t-value. Enter it here:

[   ] = tabled t-value

Interpret the t-test

If the obtained t-value is <u>greater</u> than the tabled t-value, then you have shown that the program significantly improved the scores of participants who got it. If your obtained t-value is less, then there is more than a 10% chance that the results were just due to chance. Such results are not usually considered statistically significant. The program has not been shown to make a statistically significant difference on this test.

The test of statistical significance which you have used here allows a 10% chance that you will claim a significant difference when the results were in fact only due to chance. If you want to make a firmer claim, use the Table of t-Values in Appendix B. This table allows only a 5% chance of making such an error.

A good procedure in any case is to repeat the program another cycle and again perform this evaluation by experiment—only this time, use the 5% table to test the results. If your results are again significant, you will have very strong ground for asserting that the program makes a statistically significant difference in results on the outcome measure.

Construct a Graph of Scores

If results were statistically significant, display them graphically. Figures A and B present two appropriate ways to do this. Figure A requires fewer calculations.

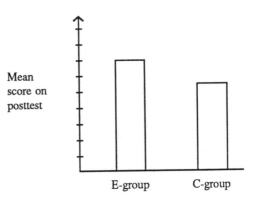

Figure A. Posttest means of groups formed from matched pairs.

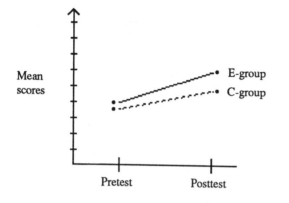

Figure B. Pretest and posttest mean scores of
experimental and control groups.

You may wish to take a closer look at the results than just examining averages or single tests of significance. Taking a
close look will further help you interpret results. In particular, if the results were not statistically significant, you may
want to look for general trends.

One good way to take a closer look at results is to compute
the gain score—posttest minus pretest—for each participant.
Using gain scores, you can plot two bar graphs, one showing
gain scores in the experimental group and the other showing
gain scores in the control or comparison group. If some participants' scores were quite extreme, look into these cases.
Perhaps there was some special condition, such as illness or
coaching, which explains extreme scores. If so, these students' scores should be dropped and the t-test for differences
in posttest scores computed again. Or there may be some
background characteristics or predisposition which seem to
be causing extreme effects. If so, these should be noted.

If your task is formative, meet with staff to discuss results

Instructions

The agenda for this meeting should have an outline something like the following:

Introduction

Review the contents of the worksheet in Step 3, pages 127 and 128.

Presentation of Results

Display and discuss the attrition table which describes participant absences from the experimental and control groups. Display Figures A and B and discuss them. Report the results of the test of significance.

Discussion of the Results

If the difference was significant as hypothesized—the E-group did better than the C-group—you will need to answer these questions:

- Was the result practically significant? That is, was the difference between the E-group and the C-group large enough to be of practical value?
- Were the results heavily influenced by a few dramatic gains or losses?
- Were the gains worth the effort involved in implementing the program?

If the results were nonsignificant, you will need to consider:

- Do you think this was due to too short a time span to give the program a fair chance to show its effects, or was the program a poor one?
- Were there special problems which could be remedied?
- Was the result nearly significant?
- Should the program be tried again, perhaps with improvements?

Recommendations

On the basis of the results, what recommendations can be made? Should the program be expanded? Should another evaluation be conducted to get firmer results—perhaps using more students? Can the program be improved? Could the evaluation be improved? Collect and discuss recommendations.

Write a report if necessary

Instructions

Use as resources the book How to Communicate Evaluation Findings and the worksheet in Step 3 of this guide. The worksheet, you will remember, contains an early draft of the sections of the report that describe the program and the evaluation.

You have reached the end of the Step-by-Step Guide for Conducting a Small Experiment. Two appendices follow:

- Appendix A contains an example of an evaluation report prepared using this guide.

- Appendix B contains the table of values for performing a t-test of statistical significance at the 5% level.

Example of an Evaluation Report

This example—which is fictitious and should not be interpreted as evidence for or against any particular counseling method—illustrates how an experiment can form the nucleus of an evaluation. Notice that information from the experiment does not form the sole content of the report. The evaluator has to consider many contextual, program-specific pieces of information, such as the exact nature of the program, the possible bias that might be introduced into the data by the information available to the respondents, etc. There is no substitute for thoughtfulness and common sense in interpreting an evaluation.

EVALUATION REPORT

Program	The Preventive Counseling Program
Program location	Naughton High School
Evaluator	J. P. Simon, Principal Naughton High School
Report submitted to	J. Ross, Director of Evaluation Mimieux School District
Period covered by report	January 6, 19xx-February 16, 19xx
Date report submitted	March 31, 19xx

Section I. Summary

A new counseling technique based on "reality therapy" and the motto that "prevention is better than cure" was developed by the Mimieux School District and consultants.

Naughton High School evaluated this Preventive Counseling program by making it available to one group of students, but not to a matched control group.

Results of teacher ratings subsequent to the Preventive Counseling program and a count of the number of referrals to the office, both pointed to the success of the Preventive Counseling program at least on this short-term basis.

This evaluation report details these findings and presents a series of recommendations for further evaluation of this promising program.

Section II. Background Information Concerning the Preventive Counseling Program

A. Origin of the Program

Several counselors had received special training, at district expense, in a style of counseling related to "reality therapy." This counseling was designed to be used with students whom teachers felt were "heading for trouble" in school or not adjusting well to school life. By an intensive course of counseling, it was hoped to prevent future problems, hence the title the Preventive Counseling program. The district office asked Naughton High School to assess the effectiveness of this kind of counseling. A counselor trained in the technique was made available to the school on a trial basis for four hours a day over a two-week period.

B. Goal of the Program

The goal of the Preventive Counseling (PC) program was to promote successful adjustment to school among students whom teachers referred to the office.

C. Characteristics of the Program

In the PC program, a student who is referred by a teacher receives an initial 20 minutes of counseling. Follow-up counseling sessions are given to the student each day for the next two weeks.

This program differs from methods used previously to handle referrals to the office. Previously, teachers were not encouraged to refer students to the office. When a student was referred for some particular reason, he generally received one counseling session and perhaps no follow-up at all, unless the teacher referred the student again. This kind of counseling was the responsibility of the usual counseling staff or, in exceptional cases, the vice-principal.

The PC program:

1. Uses counselors who are specially trained in "reality therapy" counseling

2. Requests referrals before an incident necessitates referral

3. Gives the student two weeks of counseling

D. Students Involved in the Program

The counseling is appropriate for students of all grade levels. Any student referred by a teacher is eligible for counseling. During the trial period for this evaluation, however, only some referred students could receive the PC program.

E. Faculty and Others Involved in the Program

As far as possible, the counselor and teachers communicated directly regarding students in need of counseling. A clerk handled scheduling of counseling sessions, managing this in addition to his other duties.

Section III. Description of the Evaluation Study

A. Purposes of the Evaluation

The District Office wanted Naughton High School to evaluate the effectiveness of the new style of counseling. The study in this school was to be one of several studies conducted to assist the District in deciding whether or not to have other counselors receive reality therapy training and conduct preventive counseling.

Several School Board members had emphasized that they were interested in seeing firm evidence, not opinions.

B. Evaluation Design

In view of the costly decisions to be made and the desire of the Board members for "hard data," the evaluation was designed to measure the results of the PC program as objectively and accurately as possible. To accomplish this, it was deemed necessary to use a true control group. Teachers were asked to name students in their classes who were in need of counseling. For each student named, the teacher provided a rating of the student's adjustment to school on a 5-point scale from "extremely poor" to "needs a little improvement." This was called the adjustment rating.

Students referred by three of more teachers formed the sample used in the evaluation. An average adjustment rating was calculated for each of the sample students by adding together all ratings for a student and dividing by the number of ratings for that student. These students were then grouped by grade and sex. Matched pairs were formed by matching students (within a group) with close to the same average ratings.

From these matched pairs, students were randomly assigned to receive the new counseling (the Experimental or E-group) or to be the Control group or C-group. Should students from the Control group be referred for counseling because of some incident, for example, then the regular counselors were requested to counsel as they had in the past. The E-group students received the two weeks of counseling which is characteristic of the PC program.

At the end of the two-week cycle, all referrals to the office were again dealt with by regular counselors or the vice-principal. Over the next four weeks, records of referrals to the office were kept. If the number of referrals to the office was significantly fewer for the students who had received the PC program (i.e., the E-group students), then the program would be inferred to have been successful.

This measure is reasonably objective and the random assignment of students from matched pairs ensured the initial similarity of the two groups, thus making is possible to conclude that any difference in subsequent rates was due to the PC program.

C. Outcome Measures

As mentioned above, the effect of the program was measured by counting, from office records, how many times each control group student and how many times each experimental group student was referred to the office in the four weeks after the intervention program ended.

An unavoidable problem was that teachers were sometimes aware of which students had been receiving the regular counseling, since students were called to the office regularly for two weeks from their classes. Teachers might have been influenced by this fact. In order to reduce the possible impact of this situation on teacher referral behavior, the fact that the evaluation was being conducted was not made known until after the data collection period was over (four weeks after the Preventive Counseling program ended).

A second measure of outcomes was also collected: teachers were asked at the end of the data collection period to re-rate all students previously identified as needing counseling, giving a "student adjustment rating" on the same 5-point scale which had been used in the beginning of the program.

D. Implementation Measures

The counselor's records provided the documentation for the program. Essentially, these records were used to verify that only E-group students had received the Preventive Counseling program and to record any absences which might require that the student not be counted in the evaluation results.

Section IV. Results

A. Results of Implementation Measures

Eighteen pairs of students were formed from teachers' referrals. The 18 students in the E-group had a perfect attendance record during the Preventive Counseling program and did not miss any counseling sessions. However, two students in the control group were absent for a week. These students and their matched pairs were not counted in the analysis thus leaving a total of 16 matched pairs.

B. Results of Outcome Measures

Table 1 shows the number of referrals to the office from the experimental and control groups during each of the four weeks following the end of the PC program.

TABLE 1
Number of Referrals to the Office

	# of referrals to office				
	Week 1	Week 2	Week 3	Week 4	Total
E-group (had received PC)	1	1	1	2	5
C-group (had not received PC)	3	2	3	2	10

There were twice as many referrals (10 as opposed to 5) in the control group as in the experimental group. Closer analysis revealed that 4 of the referrals in the E-group were produced by one student who was referred to the office each week. Checking the number of students referred at least once (as opposed to the total number of referrals), it was found that there were two for the experimental and six for the control group.

The second set of averaged school adjustment ratings collected from teachers is recorded in Figure 1, and the calculations for a test of the significance of the results are presented in the same figure. The t-test for correlated means was used to examine the hypothesis that the E-group's average adjustment ratings would be higher, after the program, than those of the C-group. The hypothesis could be accepted with only a 10% chance that the obtained difference was simply the result of chance sampling fluctuations. The obtained t-value was 2.06, and the tabled t-value (.10 level) was 1.34.

Data Sheet

E-group		C-group				
Student	Final average adjustment rating	Student	Final average adjustment rating	d	$(d-\bar{d})$	$(d-\bar{d})^2$
AK	3	WK	1	2	1.38	1.90
GF	2	LJ	2	0	- .62	0.38
ST	4	CF	1	3	2.38	5.66
CT	4	LM	3	1	0.38	0.14
JB	3	MH	3	0	-0.62	0.38
SK	3	FH	4	-1	-1.62	2.62
UL	5	DH	5	0	-0.62	0.38
MQ	5	RR	4	1	0.38	0.14
JJ	3	XT	1	2	1.38	1.90
WV	2	KN	2	0	- .62	0.38
AC	4	JR	3	1	0.38	0.14
CK	3	OF	4	-1	-1.62	2.62
CR	2	PD	1	1	0.38	0.14
RA	5	NW	5	0	-0.62	0.38
PG	3	JM	4	-1	-1.62	2.62
FW	4	RL	2	2	1.38	1.90
n = 16				10		21.68

$$\bar{d} = \frac{13-3}{16} \qquad s_d = \sqrt{\frac{21.68}{15}}$$

$$= \frac{10}{16} \qquad\qquad = \sqrt{1.44}$$

$$\boxed{\sqrt{n} = 4} \qquad \boxed{\bar{d} = 0.62} \qquad \boxed{s_d = 1.20}$$

$$t = \frac{(\bar{d})\,(\sqrt{n})}{s_d}$$

$$t = \frac{(0.62)\,(4)}{1.20} = \frac{2.48}{1.20} = \boxed{2.06}$$

Figure 1

C. Informal Results

Several teachers commented informally about the counseling that their problem students were receiving. One said the counseling seemed to be less "touchy feely" and more "getting down to specifics," and she noted an increase in task orientation in a counselee in her room beginning at about the second week of special counseling. She felt, however, that the counseling should have continued longer. Other teachers did not seem to have ascertained the style of counseling being used, but commented that counseling seemed to be having less transitory effect than usual.

A parent of one of the counselees in the PC program called the principal to praise the consistent help his child was getting from the special counselor. "I think this might turn him around," the parent said.

Negative comments came from one teacher who complained that one of her students always seemed to miss some important activity by being summoned to the counseling sessions. Another teacher, however, commented that it was a relief to have the counselee gone for a little while each day.

Section V. Discussion of Results

The use of a true experimental design enables the results reported above to be interpreted with some confidence. Initially, the E-group and C-group were composed of very similar students because of the procedure of matching and random assignment. The E-group received Preventive Counseling whereas the C-group did not. In the four weeks following the program, all students were in their regular programs and during this time, students from the C-group received twice as many referrals to the office as students from the E-group.

In interpreting this measure, it should be remembered that referral to the office is a quite objective behavioral measure of the effect of the program. It appears that the Preventive Counseling program substantially reduced the number of referrals to the office over this four-week period. Whether this difference will continue is not known at this time.

The average post-counseling ratings which teachers assigned to students in the E-group and in the C-group showed a significant difference in favor of the E-group. A problem in interpreting this result is that the teachers were aware of which students had been in the counseling program and this might have affected their ratings. However, 52 teachers were involved in these ratings, some rating only one student and others rating more. That the result was in the same direction as the behavioral measure lends both measures additional credibility.

Section VI. Cost-Benefit Considerations

The program appears to have an initially beneficial effect. However, it also is a fairly expensive program. There are two main expenses involved: the cost of training counselors in reality therapy and the cost of providing the counseling time in the school. There was no way in this evaluation of determining if the training had an important influence on the program's effectiveness. It could have been that other program characteristics—its preventive approach or the continuous daily counseling—were the influential characteristics. Training in reality therapy could possibly be dispensed with, thus saving some of the expense. However, since training can presumably have lasting effects on a counselor, its cost over the long run is not great and comes nowhere near approaching the cost of the provision of counseling time each day.

It is understood that a cost-benefit analysis will be conducted by the District office using results from several schools. One question needing consideration is whether the Preventive Counseling program will in fact save personnel time in the long run by catching minor problems before they develop into major problems. To answer such a question requires the collection of data over a longer time period than the few weeks employed in this evaluation. If the program helps students to overcome classroom problems, then its benefits—although perhaps immeasurable—might be great.

Section VII. Conclusions and Recommendations

A. Conclusions

In this small scale experiment, the Preventive Counseling program appeared to be superior to normal practice. It produced better adjustment to school, as rated by teachers, and resulted in fewer teacher referrals to the office in the four weeks following the end of the two week PC program. It was not possible to determine, from this small study, the extent to which each of the program's main characteristics was important to the success of the overall program.

B. Recommendations Regarding the Program

1. The Preventive Counseling program is promising and should be continued for further evaluation.

2. Preventive Counseling without the reality therapy training might be instituted on a trial basis.

C. Recommendations Regarding Subsequent Evaluation of the Program

1. The kind of evaluation reported here, an evaluation based on a true experiment and fairly objective

measures, should be repeated several times to check the reliability of the effects of counseling as so measured.

2. In several evaluations of the Preventive Counseling program, the outcome data should be collected over a period of several months to assess long-term effects.

3. The School Board and the schools should be provided with a cost analysis of the counseling program which includes a clear indication of (a) the alternative uses to which the money might be put were it not spent on the PC program, and (b) the cost of other means of assisting students referred by teachers.

4. An evaluation should be designed to measure the relative effectiveness of the following four programs:

   • The Preventive Counseling program

   • The Preventive Counseling program run without reality therapy training

   • Reality therapy provided to regular counselors

   • The ususal means of handling referrals

Table of t-Values for Correlated Means

Number of matched pairs	Tabled t-value for a 5% probability (one-tailed test)
6	2.01
7	1.94
8	1.89
9	1.86
10	1.83
11	1.81
12	1.80
13	1.78
14	1.77
15	1.76
16	1.75
17	1.75
18	1.74
19	1.73
20	1.73
21	1.72
22	1.72
23	1.72
24	1.71
25	1.71
26	1.71
.	.
40	1.68
.	.
120	1.65

Master Index to the Program Evaluation Kit

This index lists topics covered throughout the *Program Evaluation Kit*. Entries therefore indicate book and page number. The letter **H** stands for *Evaluator's Handbook*; **D** for *How to Design a Program Evaluation*; **I** for *How to Measure Implementation*; **A** for *How to Measure Attitudes*; **P** for *How to Measure Performance and Use Tests*; **Da** for *How to Analyze Data*; **F** for *How to Focus an Evaluation*; **C** for *How to Communicate Findings*; and **Q** for *How to Use Qualitative Methods in Evaluation*.